TABLE OF CONTENTS

TABLE OF CONTENTS

TIME TO THE QUARTER-HOUR

TIME TO THE MINUTE

TIME REVIEW

TABLE OF CONTENTS

TABLE OF CONTENTS

Time Two Ways

Show each time **two ways**.
Draw the hands on each clock face.
Write the time on each digital clock.

A.   Bessie Bear gets up at **6 o'clock**.

B.   Bernie Bear eats breakfast at **7 o'clock**.

C.   What time do you get up on school mornings?
Draw it here!

Name_____

Time Two Ways

Show each time **two ways**.
Draw the hands on each clock face.
Write the time on each digital clock.

A.   Randy Rabbit leaves for school at **8 o'clock**.

B.   Rebecca Rabbit goes out to recess at **10 o'clock**.

C.   What time do you go out for recess?
Draw it here!

Time Two Ways

Show each time **two ways**.
Draw the hands on each clock face.
Write the time on each digital clock.

A. Fernando Frog eats lunch at **12 o'clock.**

B. Fanny Frog goes to the library at **1 o'clock**.

C. What time do you eat lunch?
Draw it here!

Time Two Ways

Show each time **two ways**.
Draw the hands on each clock face.
Write the time.

A. At **9 o'clock,** Frog goes for a swim.

B. At **11 o'clock,** Frog sits on a lily pad.

C. At **12 o'clock,** Frog eats a sandwich.

Name_____

Time Stories

Read each story.
Draw the hands on each clock face.

A. At **11:00**, Mouse starts to cook. Yum-Yum! Cheese soup is good.

B. At **12 o'clock**, Mouse sets the table. Uh – oh! He drops a spoon.

C. At **7:00**, Mouse reads a book. What a funny story!

D. Time for bed. It is **9 o'clock**, and Mouse is sleepy.

Time Stories

Read each story.
Draw the hands on each clock face.

A. Rabbit is hungry. It is **6 o'clock**—time for supper and some carrot stew.

B. At **8:00,** Rabbit washes the dishes. Scrub, scrub, the pot is sticky.

C. Rabbit works in his garden. It is **4 o'clock,** and he is picking lettuce.

D. At **5:00,** Rabbit makes a lettuce salad. What a tasty meal!

Name_____

Time to the Half-Hour: Introduction

This clock face shows the time gone by since 8 o'clock.

Thirty minutes or **half an hour** has gone by.

There are 3 ways to say time to the half-hour. We say **seven thirty, thirty past seven** or **half past seven**.

_9:00_   **Half-hour later**   _9:30_

_30_____ minutes past_____9_____ o'clock

Half-hour later

_____ minutes past_____ o'clock

41

Writing Time on the Half-Hour

Half-hour later

_____

_____ minutes past

_____

_____ o'clock

Half-hour later

_____

_____ minutes past

_____

_____ o'clock

What is your dinner time?

Circle the time you eat.

5:30

4:30

6:30

7:30

Writing Time on the Half-Hour

What time is it?

half past_____

half past_____

half past_____

half past_____

half past_____

half past_____

Writing Time on the Half-Hour

Trace the **BIG MINUTE HAND** green.
Trace the **little hour hand** yellow.

Write the time on the line.

_____   _____

_____   _____

Time to the Half-Hour

Matching Digital and Face Clocks

Drawing the Hour Hand

Say the time.
Draw the **little hour hand**
on each clock.

Drawing the Hour Hand

Say the time.
Draw the **little hour hand**
on each clock.

Telling Time: Hour and Half-Hour

I'm mixing the **hour time** and
half-hour time. See if I can fool you!
Draw a line from the clock to the correct time.

3:00

3:30

4:00

6:30

7:00

7:30

4:00

5:00

6:00

Writing the Time: Practice

Sock Clocks

Draw the hands on the sock clocks.

1:30

7:00

4:30

10:00

3:30

9:30

4:00

2:30

Writing the Time: Practice

You Are My Sunshine
What time is it?

3:00 : : :

: : : :

: : : :

Name_____

Time Stories

Read each story.
Draw the hands on each clock face.

A. It is **5:30**, and the sun is coming up. Bird is ready for the day.

B. At **6:30**, Bird is looking for breakfast. Watch out, worms!

C. Bird is resting after breakfast. It is **9:30** and almost time for flying practice.

D. At **12:30**, Bird naps before lunch. Flying is hard work!

Time Lapse: Hours

Can you tell how much
time has passed?

____:____

____:____

If it started snowing at **3:00** and snowed until **6:00**,

it snowed _____ hours.

What time did the spider start spinning the web?

____:____

What time did she finish? ____:____

____:____

____:____

The spider took _____ hours to spin the web.

Time Lapse: Hours

Dad went to the grocery store.

_____:_____   _____:_____

Dad took _____ hour to buy groceries.

The teacher taught math class.

_____:_____   _____:_____

Math lasted _____ hour.

Write how much later.

_____ hours

Time Lapse: Hours

It is important to get home
when your parents expect you!

Steve went to play baseball at **3:30**.
Mom told him to be home in **2 hours**.

He should be home at _____ : _____ .

Show the time on this watch.

Tiffany went to Latonia's house to ride bikes at **10:00**.
Dad asked her to be home in **3 hours**.

She should be home at _____ : _____.

Show the time on this watch.

Name_____

Time Lapse: Hours

Kristen took her sister to the movies at **7:30**. Mom said she would meet them in **2 hours**.

She will meet them at _____ : _____.
Show the time on this clock.

Latrissa went to the library for story hour. She got there at **1:00**. She stayed **1 hour**.

Story hour should be over at _____ : _____.
Show the time Latrissa left for home.

Drawing the Hour Hand:
A Half-Hour Later

Draw the hands on each clock face.

A. At **7:00**, Bill turns on the TV.

What time is it one half-hour later?

B. At **4:00**, we all jump in the car.

What time is it one half-hour later?

C. At **12:00**, Julio and Nathan are ready to eat.

What time is it one half-hour later?

Name_____

Drawing the Hour Hand:
A Half-Hour Later

Draw the hands on each clock face.

A. At **8:00**, it starts to rain.

What time is it one half-hour later?

B. At **11:00**, the sun comes out.

What time is it one half-hour later?

C. At **3:00**, we skip home from school.

What time is it one half-hour later?

Drawing the Hour Hand: A Half-Hour Later

Draw the hands on each clock face.

A. At **6:30**, a fire engine roars down the street.

What time is it one half-hour later?

B. At **11:30**, everyone is playing in the schoolyard.

What time is it one half-hour later?

C. **At 5:30**, my dog gets out of the yard.

What time is it one half-hour later?

Name_____

Time Stories

Read each story.
Draw the hands on each clock face.

A. Tom makes a HUGE sandwich at **1:00**. He finishes the whole sandwich **one half-hour** later. What time does Tom finish the sandwich?

B. Tom gets home from school at **3:00**. He goes out to play **30 minutes** later. What time does Tom go out to play?

C. Tom goes to bed at **8:30**. He falls asleep **one half-hour** later. What time does Tom fall asleep?

Time Stories

Read each story.
Draw the hands on each clock face.

A.   Maria makes a lunch at **7:00**. She
     gets on the bus **30 minutes** later.
     What time does she get on the bus?

B.   Maria helps make dinner at **5:30**.
     Everyone eats it **one half-hour** later.
     What time does everyone eat?

C.   Maria's family plays a game at
     8:30. They stop playing **30 minutes**
     later. What time do they stop
     playing?

Name_____

Time Stories

Read each story.
Draw the hands on each clock face.

A. Li goes for a walk at **10:30**. He comes back with three friends **30 minutes** later. What time does he come back with his friends?

B. Li gets on his bike at **3:30**. He reaches the library **one half-hour** later. What time does he get to the library?

C. Li starts home at **5:00**. He gets home **30 minutes** later. What time does he get home?

Name_____

Time Two Ways

Draw the hands on each clock face.
Write the time.

A. At **1:30**, Squirrel hides seven nuts.

B. At **2:00**, Squirrel runs down the tree to find more nuts.

C. By **3:30**, Squirrel is ready for a long rest.

Name_____

Time Two Ways

Draw the hands on each clock face.
Write the time.

A.   At **5:30**, Toad hops over to visit Frog.

B.   At **6:00**, Frog and Toad are sipping
Fine Fly Tea.

C.   At **7:30**, Toad heads home, full of
tea and bug cakes.

Time Two Ways

Draw the hands on each clock face.
Write the time.

A. Maria Mouse gets to the library at **11 o'clock**. She leaves the library at **11:30**.

Gets to library   **Leaves the library**

B. Marcus Mouse gets to Pizza Palace at **3 o'clock**. He finishes his pizza at **3:30.**

Gets to Pizza Palace   **Finishes pizza**

Time Two Ways

Draw the hands on each clock face.
Write the time.

A.   Tim Toad begins planting the garden at **9 o'clock**.
     He finishes planting at **9:30**.

Begins planting   **Finishes planting**

B.   Tara Toad starts roller-skating at **10 o'clock**. She
     stops roller-skating **30 minutes after 10 o'clock**.

Starts roller-skating   **Stops roller-skating**

Time Two Ways

Draw the hands on each clock face.
Write the time.

A. Ricardo Raccoon starts his lunch at **12:00.** He finishes his lunch **30 minutes after 12:00.**

Starts lunch   **Finishes lunch**

B. Rachel Raccoon sits down at the computer at **7:00.** She gets up from the computer a **half-hour after 7:00**.

Sits down   **Gets up**

Time Stories

Read the story.
Write the time two ways.
Choose a time for everyone to eat lunch!

Bear is going on a picnic today with his brother and sister. They leave for the park at **9:00**. They get to the park at **10:00**. Bear helps carry the food to a picnic table. Then he gets out his kite. Bear flies his kite at **10:30**. Later, at _____ , everyone has a picnic lunch!

Put the story in order by writing what time Bear did each thing.

A. **Leave for the park**

B. **Get to the park**

C. **Fly kite**

D. **Eat lunch**

73

Time Stories

Read the story.
Write the time two ways.
Choose a time for everyone to go home!

Pig wakes up at **7:00**. Pig's grandmother is taking her to the zoo today! They get to the zoo at **10:30**. They walk and walk. They stop to eat at **12:30**. They walk some more. Pig and her grandmother don't get home until _____ .
They had a wonderful day!

Put the story in order by writing what time Pig did each thing.

A. _____

B. _____

C. _____

D. _____

ZOO

Name_____

Time Stories

Read the story.
Write the time two ways.
Choose a time for everyone to wake up!

It's a hot summer day. Frog and Turtle begin to walk to the lake at **11:00**. They jump into the cold water at **12:30**. They swim and dive. Then they enjoy lunch at **1:30**. They fall asleep after lunch. Later, at _____ , Frog and Turtle wake up. They hurry home!

Put the story in order by writing what time Frog and Turtle did each thing.

A. _____

B. _____

C. _____

D. _____

Time Puzzles

Read each "time clue."
Draw the hands on each clock.
Write the time.

A. It's dark outside.
   Everyone is asleep.

B. Ring, ring!
   Time to get up.

C. Here comes the school bus.
   Run, so you won't
   be late!

D. I'm hungry! Soon it will
   be time for lunch.

Time Puzzles

Read each "time clue."
Draw the hands on each clock.
Write the time.

A. School is out!
We're going home.

B. Here comes the mail!
I hope I get a letter.

C. It's getting dark.
Time to go inside.

D. It's light tonight.
Look, a big full moon!

Time Puzzles

Read each "time clue."
Draw the hands on each clock.
Write the time.

A. Sometimes I have
   homework to do.

B. Sometimes I have
   jobs to do.

C. The best time is when I can
   do just what I want to do.

D. On Saturday and Sunday,
   I play with friends.

Time to the Quarter-Hour: Introduction

Each **hour** has **60** minutes.
An **hour** has **4 quarter-hours**.
A **quarter-hour** is **15 minutes**.

This clock face shows
a quarter of an hour.

From the **12** to the
3 is **15 minutes**.

From the 12 to the 3 is 15 minutes.

_____15_____ minutes after _____8_____ o'clock

is _____8:15_____

Telling Time

Each **hour** has **4 quarter-hours**.
A **quarter-hour** is **15 minutes**.

Write the times.

    One Quarter-Hour later

9:00

9:15

_____15_____ minutes past _____9_____ o'clock

    One Quarter-Hour later

_____   _____

_____ minutes past _____ o'clock

Time to the Quarter-Hour

Telling Time

Draw the hands. Write the times.

5:15

_____ 15 minutes after

_____ 5 o'clock

10:15

_____ minutes after

_____ o'clock

2:15

_____ minutes after

_____ o'clock

9:15

_____ minutes after

_____ o'clock

Digital Clocks

Your **digital clock** has quarter-hours, too!
It also shows **15 minutes**.

Digital Clocks

Circle the correct digital time.

15 minutes past 6 is my dinner time.

Draw the minute hand with
an **orange** crayon.

Draw the hour hand
with a **purple** crayon.

_____ minutes after _____ o'clock

6:15

Telling Time

Count the numbers by 5's
to see how many minutes have passed.

_15_ minutes

after _12_

_30_ minutes

after _12_

_45_ minutes

after _12_

Telling Time

Can you speak **"clock time?"**

1. **"Quarter after"** means 15 minutes after the hour.

2. **"Half past"** means 30 minutes after the hour.

3. **"Quarter to"** means 15 minutes until the next hour.

Write the quarter-hours from this time.

_____ o'clock

quarter past _____

half past _____

quarter to _____

next hour: _____ o'clock

Telling Time

Write the time on the digital clocks.

Name_____

Time Two Ways

Draw the hands on each clock face.
Write the time.

A. Marta **begins** writing a letter **at 3:30.**
She **stops 30 minutes later.**

Begins

[:]

Stops

[:]

B. Arnold **begins** drying dishes **at 8:00.**
He **stops 15 minutes later.**

Begins

[:]

Stops

[:]

C. Write your own time story.

_____

_____

_____

Begins

[:]

Stops

[:]

Time Two Ways

Draw the hands on each clock face.
Write the time.

A. Darius **begins** throwing balls for the dog **at 5:00.**
He **stops 15 minutes later.**

Begins

:

Stops

:

B. Olga **begins** playing frisbee **at 4:15.**
She **stops 15 minutes later.**

Begins

:

Stops

:

C. Write your own story.

_____

_____

_____

Begins

:

Stops

:

Time to the Quarter-Hour

Time Two Ways

Draw the hands on each clock face.
Write the times.

A. Alberto begins working in the yard **at 10:00**.
He **stops 45 minutes later**.

Begins

Stops

B. Darlene begins playing catch **at 2:30**.
She **stops 15 minutes later.**

Begins

Stops

C. Write your own story.

_____

_____

Begins

Stops

Name_____

Time Two Ways

Draw the hands on each clock face.

Write the times.

A. Lucia **begins** practicing for the play **at 3:00.**
She **stops 45 minutes later.**

Begins

| : |

Stops

| : |

B. Ann **begins** sorting her baseball cards **at 7:30.**
She **stops 15 minutes later.**

Begins

| : |

Stops

| : |

C. **Solve this time puzzle.**
When did Ray begin biking?

Ray biked **for 30 minutes.**
He stopped biking **at 5:30.**

Began

| : |

Stopped

| : |

Name_____

Time Two Ways

Draw the hands on each clock face.

Write the times.

A. Jake **begins** playing a game **at 1:30.**
He **stops 45 minutes later.**

Begins

| : |

Stops

| : |

B. Nicole **begins** swim practice **at 4:45.**
She **stops 15 minutes later.**

Begins

| : |

Stops

| : |

C. **Solve this time puzzle.**
When did Jill begin working in the recycling
center? Jill worked in the recycling center
for 45 minutes. She stopped working **at 7:45.**

Began

| : |

Stopped

| : |

93

Name_____

Time to the Minute Intervals: Introduction

Each number on the clock face **stands for 5 minutes.**

Count by 5's beginning at 12
Write the numbers here:

00   05   10   15   20   25

It is __25__ minutes after __8__ o'clock. **It is written 8:25.**

Count by 5's.

00   ___   ___   ___   ___   ___   ___   ___

It is _____ minutes after _____ o'clock.

_____ : _____

Time to the Minute Intervals: Introduction

Write the time both ways.

00 _____ _____

_____ minutes after _____ o'clock

_____ : _____

---

00 _____ _____ _____ _____

_____ minutes after _____ o'clock

_____ : _____

---

00 _____ _____ _____ _____ _____

_____ _____

_____ minutes after _____ o'clock

_____ : _____

---

00 _____ _____ _____ _____ _____

_____ _____

_____ minutes after _____ o'clock

_____ : _____

Circle the clocks with times between 3 o'clock and 9 o'clock.

Telling Time by 5 Minutes
(Use with page 97)

2:20

6:15

4:50

11:45

9:35

12:30

7:05

5:10

Telling Time by 5 Minutes

These clock faces got lost from their clocks.
Can you help put them together again?

Read the time on each clock face.
Find the clock on page 96 with the correct time.
Cut out the face and glue it on the clock.

**This page left blank for
cutting lesson on reverse side.**

Name_____

Drawing the Minute Hand

This clock lost its minute hand!
Can you help it?

Read the time.
Draw the minute hand with a pencil.
Color over it with a **red** crayon.

2:05

____5____ minutes after ____2____ o'clock

Drawing the Minute Hand

Draw and color the minute hand.

12:25

1:20

11:15

3:50

5:30

10:35

Drawing the Minute Hand

Fish Time
Draw the hands on these fish clocks.

7:45   8:05   11:15

3:20   5:55   1:50

12:10   10:25   4:40

Drawing the Minute Hand

Cartoon Time!
Draw the clock hands
to show the time you
watch these cartoons.

Space Bunny 7:35	Car Wars 8:45	The Snuffs 5:15

Space Bunny
7:35

Car Wars
8:45

The Snuffs
5:15

Fun Runner
9:00

Scare Bears
2:40

Magic Elf
11:30

Tummy Bears
3:20

Monster Time
12:10

Sunny Funnies
1:05

What is your favorite cartoon? _____

What time does it come on?_____

Digital Clocks

Can you read a digital clock?
First read the hour.
Then read the minutes.

This clock is read **four twenty
or twenty minutes past 4 o'clock.**

Match the digital and face clocks.

Digital Clocks

Circle the words to match the times.

five twenty five fifty

six twenty-five six thirty-five

seven ten seven twenty

one fifty-five eleven fifty-five

Matching Digital and Face Clocks

Clock Tower Times

Cut out and glue under the correct clock.

12:35	8:40	4:15	9:55	10:05
6:10	1:45	12:20	2:45	3:25

Writing the Time

Apple Time

Write the times on the worms.

Time Two Ways

Draw the hands on each clock face.
Write the time.

A. 2 hours past midnight

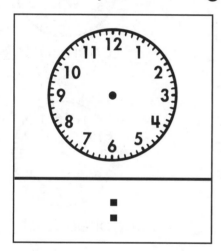

B. 10 minutes after 2:00

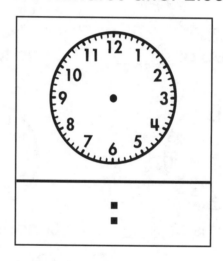

C. 45 minutes after 2:00

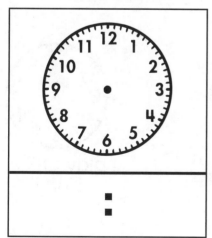

D. 50 minutes before 3:00

Name_____

Writing Familiar Times:
Family "Time Tree"

Write the time.
Draw the hands on each clock.

I get up at _____.   I go to bed at _____.   Lunch is at _____.

Dinner is at _____.   School starts at _____.   School ends at _____.

Recess is at _____.   I play at _____.

Name_____

Time Lapse: Minutes

Our school had an "end-of-school picnic."
We really had fun!

How much time did each activity take?

1. Jimmy played darts from 1:20 till 1:40.
   He played for __20__ minutes.

2. Marietta rode a pony for 15 minutes.
   She began at 1:00.
   She finished at ____ : _____ .

3. She had so much fun, she rode
   another 15 minutes.
   She finished at ____ : _____ .

Name_____

Time Lapse: Minutes

4. Tim worked at the snow cone booth. The first clock shows the time he started. He worked 1 hour and 30 minutes. **Show the time** he finished on the second clock.

5. Andrea won the juggling contest. She kept the balls in the air for 5 minutes. She began juggling at 1:25. She finished at _____ : _____.
Circle the clock which shows the correct time.

Keep it up!

Write the time.

_____   _____   _____   _____

Time to the Minute

Drawing Clock Hands

Show the Times

Read each story.
Draw the hands on each clock face.

A. Frog sees a fly at 1:00. He catches the fly and
   eats it 60 minutes later.

Sees fly   **Eats fly**

B. Frog hops out of the water at 2:00.
   Frog hops back in the water 40 minutes later.

Hops out   **Hops back in**

C. Frog sits on a lily pad at 3:00.
   He swims away 45 minutes later.

Sits on lily pad   **Swims away**

115

Drawing Clock Hands

Show the Times
Read each story.
Draw the hands on each clock face.

A. Rabbit hops into his garden at 6:00. He finishes
working in the garden one and one-half hours later.

Hops in garden   Finishes work

B. Rabbit gets out lettuce and carrots at 8:30.
He finishes eating 45 minutes later.

Gets out lettuce & carrots   Finishes eating

C. Rabbit lies down for a nap at 4:00. He wakes
up and hip-hops away 55 minutes later.

Lies down   Wakes up

Name_____

Drawing Clock Hands

Show the Times
Read each story.
Draw the hands on each clock face.

A. Pig takes a mud bath at 9:00.
   Pig showers off 15 minutes later.

Takes mud bath   **Showers off**

B. On Monday, Pig begins cleaning at noon.
   Her house is clean and neat 90 minutes later.

Begins cleaning   **House is clean**

C. On Tuesday, Pig goes to the market at 12:45.
   She comes home with a basket full of goodies
   30 minutes later.

Goes to market   **Comes home**

Time Stories

Read the story.
Write the times on each digital clock.

Val and Phil Camp Out

Val and Phil go out to the backyard at 6:00.
They put up their tent. This takes them 1 hour and 30
minutes. They get in the tent and talk for 1 hour.
Then they fall asleep. They sleep for 2 hours, until
a dog barks and wakes them up.

A. Go to backyard

```
  :
```

B. Finish putting up tent

```
  :
```

C. Fall asleep

```
  :
```

D. Dog barks

```
  :
```

E. How long are Val and Phil in the yard before the
dog wakes them up?

_____ hours _____ minutes

Time Stories

Read the story.
Write the times on each digital clock.

Mike and Maria Go Skating

Mike and Maria leave home at 3:30. They ride their bikes to the ice-skating rink. This takes one half-hour. They skate and leave the rink 2 hours later. They get on their bikes and arrive home 40 minutes after leaving the rink.

A. Leave home

```
:
```

B. Get to rink

```
:
```

C. Leave rink

```
:
```

D. Arrive home

```
:
```

E. How long does Mike & Maria's trip to the skating rink and back take?

_____ hours _____ minutes

Time Stories

Read the story.
Write the times on each digital clock.

Joe and José Go Skating

Joe and José put on roller skates at 8:30. They skate for 2 hours, then stop to rest. They rest for one half-hour, then start skating again. They reach the park 1 hour and 45 minutes later.

A. Put on roller skates

```
┌──────────┐
│    ■     │
│    ■     │
└──────────┘
```

B. Stop to rest

```
┌──────────┐
│    ■     │
│    ■     │
└──────────┘
```

C. Start skating again

```
┌──────────┐
│    ■     │
│    ■     │
└──────────┘
```

D. Get to park

```
┌──────────┐
│    ■     │
│    ■     │
└──────────┘
```

E. How long does Joe and José's trip to the park take?
_____ hours _____ minutes

Name_____

Time Stories

Read each time story.
Write the time on each clock.

Andrea took her dog for a walk. They left home at 5:30. They walked for 20 minutes. What time did they get home?

A. Leave home

B. Get home

Rhiannon and her mother were making cookies. They put the cookies in the oven at 7:15. After 10 minutes they took the cookies out of the oven. Yum! What time did they take them out?

C. Cookies in oven

D. Cookies out of oven

Solve the time puzzle.
When did Anita begin playing ping-pong? Anita played ping-pong with her brother for 30 minutes. They stopped playing at 4:30.

E. Begin playing

F. Stop playing

Time Stories

Read each time story.
Write the time on each clock.

Benito went for a ride on the roller coaster. He got on the roller coaster at 2:30. He rode for 15 minutes. What time did he get off?

A. Start ride

B. Get off

Valerie and her sister went hiking. They started hiking at 9:00. They hiked for one hour and 30 minutes. What time did they stop hiking?

C. Start hike

D. Finish hike

Solve this time puzzle.
When did Ben and his mother get on the subway?
Ben and his mother rode the subway for 20 minutes.
They got off the subway at 4:30.

E. Get on

F. Get off

Time Stories

Read each time story.
Write the time on each clock.

Andrea and her sister walked by the lake. They started walking at 2:15. They walked for one hour and 15 minutes. What time did they stop walking?

A. Start walking

B. Stop walking

Berta gave her dog Maria a bath. She started washing Maria at 7:40. Maria hates baths. It took Berta 50 minutes to wash the dog. They both got wet! When did she finish?

C. Start bath

D. Finish bath

Solve this time puzzle.
When did Sergei start playing frisbee? Sergei played frisbee with his brother for 40 minutes. They stopped playing at 7:30.

E. Start playing

F. Stop playing

Name_____

Time Puzzles

Write any time that fits the time clues.

A. Between 11:00 and 12:00

```
┌──────────────┐
│     ■        │
│     ■        │
└──────────────┘
```

B. Between 30 minutes after 2:00 and 3:00

```
┌──────────────┐
│     ■        │
│     ■        │
└──────────────┘
```

C. After quarter-past 7:00 and before 8:00

```
┌──────────────┐
│     ■        │
│     ■        │
└──────────────┘
```

D. **Make up** your own time clues.
   Ask a friend to solve your time puzzle!

_____

_____

_____

7:15 is my bedtime.

Name_____

Time Puzzles

Write any time that fits the time clues.

A. Between 4:15 and 5:15

B. After 6:00 and before quarter to 7:00

Time to brush my teeth!

6:45

C. Between noon and 1:00

D. **Make up** your own time clues.
   Ask a friend to solve your time puzzle!

_____

_____

_____

125

Name_____

Time Puzzles

Write any time that fits the time clues.

A. After 3:00 and before 3:40

It's lunchtime!

B. Between quarter after 1:00 and 3:00

C. Before 9:00 and after 8:20

D. **Make up** your own time clues.
   Ask a friend to solve your time puzzle!

_____

_____

_____

126

Name_____

Time Stories

Read the story. **Write** the time on each clock.

Story Times

Erin and her brother Harry were shopping for dinner. First they went into the bakery at 5:00 to buy fresh bread. This took 5 minutes. Next they walked to the market for vegetables and cereal. This took them 20 minutes. Then they walked next door for a treat at Fanny's Famous Fudge. This took them 15 minutes. Then they met their brother Andrew outside.

A. Go into bakery

C. Leave bakery

B. Leave market

D. See Andrew

E. How long had Erin and Harry been shopping when they saw Andrew?

_____

F. Make up your own story about shopping. What do you do, and how long does each thing take? Make up a starting time. Use your clock to find the ending time.

Time Stories

Read the story. **Write** the time on each clock.

Story Times

Hanna and Shawn got to the fair at 3:00. They threw balls at the clown's pocket for 10 minutes. No luck! Then they rode the Big Dipper for 30 minutes. They got wet! After this they ate pizza for 15 minutes. Then they saw their friend Mary.

A. Go to fair

B. Stop throwing balls

C. Stop riding Big Dipper

D. See Mary

E. How long had Hanna and Shawn been at the fair when they saw Mary?

_____

F. Make up your own story about being at a fair. What do you do, and how long does each thing take? Make up a starting time. Use your clock to find the ending time.

Name_____

Time Stories

Read the story. **Write** the time on each clock.

Story Times

A. Valerie and Angela got off the bus at the mall. It was 12:30. First they went to Toby's Toys & Games. They looked at toys for 20 minutes. Then they spent 40 minutes walking to Yummy Yogurt and having a snack. Then they looked at shoes in The Shoe Factory for 15 minutes. They met Angela's sister outside the Shoe Factory.

A. Go to mall

B. Leave toy store

 C. Leave Yummy Yogurt   **D.** See Angela's sister

E. How long had Valerie and Angela been at the mall when they saw Angela's sister?

_____

F. Make up your own story about being at a mall. What do you do, and how long does each thing take? Make up a starting time. Use your clock to find the ending time.

Telling Time: Using Charts

BIG TEN MOVIES:

Mark's Great Adventure	12:15	3:00	5:30
The Mad Hatter Returns	12:45	3:30	5:45
Morris and the Magic Van	1:30	4:15	6:45

Use the chart.

Write the time that each pair went to a movie.

A. Barry and his brother went to the movie that began closest to 4:00.

Movie: _____

Began at: _____

B. Andrea and her friend went to the movie that began closest to 1:00.

Movie: _____

Began at: _____

C. Ismelda and her mom went to the movie that began closest to 6:00.

Movie: _____

Began at: _____

D. **Make up** your own time puzzle about Big Ten Movies.

Telling Time: Using Charts

MAIN AIRPORT

MONDAY DEPARTURES:

Gull Air	10:45	12:10	1:45
Far West Airlines	9:25	10:10	11:40
Swift Flights	12:30	1:15	2:20

Use the chart.
Write the time that each pair took a flight.

A. Teresa and her aunt flew on the plane that left closest to 10:30.
   Airline: _____
   Left at: _____

B. Kelly and her mother flew on the plane that left closest to 11:00.
   Airline: _____
   Left at: _____

C. Leticia and her father flew on the plane that left closest to 12:15.
   Airline: _____
   Left at: _____

D. **Make up** your own time puzzle about the Main Airport.

Name_____

Telling Time: Using Charts

BAYSIDE AQUARIUM

SATURDAY FEEDINGS:

Otters	2:00	3:30	5:00
Dolphins	11:30	3:15	5:20
Sharks	2:30	4:00	5:45

Use the chart.

Write the time that each pair went to a feeding.

A. Francisco and José went to the feeding that was closest to 3:00.

Animal: _____

Feeding at: _____

B. Alex and Shannon went to the feeding that was closest to 6:00.

Animal: _____

Feeding at: _____

C. Kim and Amanda went to the feeding that was closest to 5:30.

Animal: _____

Feeding at: _____

D. **Make up** your own time puzzle about the Bayside Aquarium.

Counting Pennies

Count the pennies in each triangle.

_____ ¢

_____ ¢

_____ ¢

Don't knock the pennies down!

Counting Pennies

I put my pennies in bags.

Write the number of pennies on each bag.
Color each penny.

...the merry-go-round?

_____ ¢

...the water flume?

_____ ¢

...the bumper cars?

_____ ¢

Counting Pennies

A **penny** is worth **1¢**.
Count the money. How much?

A.

_____ ¢

B.

_____ ¢

Counting Pennies

Count the money. How much? ____

A.

_____ ¢

B.

_____ ¢

Counting Pennies
Who Has More Money?

Count the money.
Write the amount.

A.

_____¢

B.

_____¢

C. Circle the answer.
Who has more money?

Name_____

Counting with Nickels and Pennies

Who Has More Money?

Count the money.
Write the amount.

A.

_____ ¢

B.

_____ ¢

C. **Circle** the answer.
Who has more money?

157

Name_____

Counting with
Nickels and Pennies

Each **nickel** is worth **5 cents**.
Show how much these nickels are worth.

 = _____ ¢

 = _____ ¢

= _____ ¢ = _____ ¢

 = _____ ¢

= _____ ¢

= _____ ¢ = _____ ¢

 = _____ ¢

= _____ ¢

= _____ ¢

= _____ ¢ = _____ ¢

Counting with Nickels and Pennies

Who Has More Money?

Count the money.
Write the amount. _____

A.

_____ ¢

B.

_____ ¢

C. **Circle** the answer.
Who has more money?

Nickels: Counting By Fives

Let's count my nickels to see if we have enough to buy something!

Count by 5's.

See how far you can count.

__5__ , __10__ , __15__ , __20__ , __25__ ,

__30__ , __35__ , __40__ , __45__ , __50__ ,

__55__ , __60__ , __65__ , __70__ , __75__ ,

__80__ , __85__ , __90__ , __95__ , __100__ ,

This is how to count nickels!

Practice counting by 5's!

Nickels: Counting By Fives

Nickel Pickles
Count the nickels by 5's.
5 cents = 1 nickel

Write the amount.
Example:

15 ¢

PICKLES 5¢ each

Count _5_, _10_, _15_.

☐ ¢

Count ____, ____.

☐ ¢

Count ____, ____, ____,
____, ____.

☐ ¢

Count ____, ____, ____, ____,
____, ____, ____.

☐ ¢

Count ____, ____, ____,
____.

☐ ¢

Count ____, ____, ____,
____, ____, ____.

Nickels: Counting By Fives

Clowns

Count the nickels.
How much money is each clown worth?

_____ ¢

_____ ¢

_____ ¢

_____ ¢

Nickels: Counting By Fives

Feed the Meter

Count the nickels.
Write the money in the meter.

Example:

Nickels: Counting By Fives

Five Hive

How much money is in each hive?

Example:

5¢
5¢
5¢
5¢ __20__ ¢

5¢
5¢
5¢
5¢
5¢ **25** ¢

5¢
5¢ **10** ¢

5¢
5¢
5¢
5¢
5¢
5¢ **30** ¢

5¢
5¢
5¢ **15** ¢

5¢ **5** ¢

5¢
5¢
5¢
5¢
5¢
5¢
5¢ **35** ¢

5¢
5¢
5¢
5¢
5¢
5¢
5¢
5¢
5¢
5¢ ____ ¢

5¢
5¢
5¢
5¢
5¢
5¢
5¢
5¢
5¢ ____ ¢

Name_____

Name _____

Counting with Nickels and Pennies

"Cent"-erpillars

Count the coins on each "cent"-erpillar.

Example:

17 ¢

_____ ¢

_____ ¢

_____ ¢

_____ ¢

_____ ¢

_____ ¢

_____ ¢

_____ ¢

_____ ¢

_____ ¢

_____ ¢

Counting with Nickels and Pennies

Count the money.
Start with nickels. Then **count** the pennies.

A. __5__ ¢ __1__ ¢ __1__ ¢ __1__ ¢ = __8__ ¢
                                        Total

B. __5__ ¢ __1__ ¢ __1__ ¢ __1__ ¢ __1__ ¢ __1__ ¢ __1__ ¢

= __11__ ¢
   Total

C. __5__ ¢ __1__ ¢ __1__ ¢ __1__ ¢ __1__ ¢

= __9__ ¢
   Total

Counting with Nickels and Pennies

Look at the price on each toy.
Color it if there are enough nickels.

 25¢

 30¢

 20¢

 35¢

Good counting!

Name_____

Adding with
Nickels and Pennies

Adding money is **fun and easy!**

Write how much money there is in all.

☐ ¢

+

☐ ¢

_____

☐ ¢ in
all

☐ ¢ + ☐ ¢ = ☐ ¢

Adding with
Nickels and Pennies

Draw groups of pennies and nickels here.
Write an addition sentence using the
coins you drew. **Color the coins.**

You are catching on!

Adding with Nickels and Pennies

Go Bananas over Money!
Write an addition sentence for each problem.

Example:

2¢ + 1¢ = 3¢
_____

_____

_____

_____

_____

_____

_____

_____

_____

_____

172

Adding with Nickels and Pennies

Kristen is having a birthday party. Let's see what she bought for her 3 friends.

 5¢   **3¢**   **2¢**

 4¢   **2¢**   **1¢**

These are for her friends.

1. For Cassie, she bought the and the .

   She paid _____¢.

2. For Terri, she bought the and the .

   She paid _____¢.

3. For Lauren, she bought the and the .

   She paid _____¢.

Adding with
Nickels and Pennies

Every birthday party needs balloons.
Draw one for each girl, including Kristen.

They cost 5¢ each. **Count** by 5's. She paid _____ ¢.

She also bought bubble wands.
Draw one for each girl.

They cost 2¢ each. **Count** by 2's. She paid _____ ¢.

Finally! The presents!
Color the presents.

Name_____

Dimes: Introduction

You have met some of my
friends – Penny and Nickel.
Now, meet Dime!

My friend Dime is small, but quite strong.
It can buy more than Penny or Nickel.

front

back

Each side of a dime is different. It has ridges on its
edge. Color the dime silver.

 =

_____ dime = _____ pennies

_____ dime = _____ cents

_____ dime = _____ ¢

Counting with Dimes and Pennies

When Dime and his penny friends go together,
they are easy to count.

 +   = _____ ¢

Say _____   _____ _____

Always begin with the dime, then add the pennies.

 +   = _____ ¢

_____   _____ _____ _____

 + = _____ ¢

_____   _____

 +

_____   _____ _____ _____

   = _____ ¢

_____ _____ _____

Counting with Dimes and Nickels

Do you like to do tricks?

I want to show you a trick about
counting dimes and nickels.

Look carefully at these dimes and nickels.
Circle two nickels, then two more,
until all the nickels are circled.

Then **count** by 10's to see how much money is here.

I see _____ ¢

Counting with Dimes and Nickels

Count the money.
Start with dimes, then **count** the nickels.

Write the amount.

A.

____¢   ____¢   ____¢   ____¢   ____¢   ____¢
                                          Total

B.

____¢   ____¢   ____¢   ____¢   ____¢   ____¢

____¢   ____¢   ____¢   ____¢
                         Total

C. Solve this puzzle.
What coins does
Raccoon have?

I'm counting my money.
10¢, 20¢, 30¢, 35¢,
40¢, 45¢, 50¢...

Counting with Dimes, Nickels and Pennies

Count the money.
Start with the dime.

Write the amount.

A.

_____¢

B.

_____¢

C. **Circle** the answer.
Who has more money?

Counting with
Dimes, Nickels and Pennies

Count the money.
Start with the dime.

Write the amount.

A. _____ ¢

B. _____ ¢

C. _____ ¢

Counting with Dimes, Nickels and Pennies

Count the money.
Start with the dime.

Write the amount.

A.

_____¢

B.

_____¢

Counting with Dimes, Nickels and Pennies

Count the money.
Start with the dime.
Then **count** the nickels and pennies.

Write the amount.

A.

_____ ¢

B.

_____ ¢

Counting with Dimes, Nickels and Pennies

Count the money.

Write the amount.

A.

_____ ¢

B.

_____ ¢

Counting with
Dimes, Nickels and Pennies

Money Belts

Count the money on each belt.
Write the amount under the belt.

Example:

$$\underline{16¢}$$

_____ ¢

_____ ¢

_____ ¢

_____ ¢

_____ ¢

_____ ¢

_____ ¢

_____ ¢

_____ ¢

_____ ¢

Counting with Dimes, Nickels and Pennies

The children made block towers.

Circle the block in each set with the greater amount.

Counting with
Dimes, Nickels and Pennies

Write how many cents.

1.   _____ ¢

2.   _____ ¢

3.   _____ ¢

If you add 1 more penny to
number 1, you will have   _____ ¢

If you add 1 more penny to
number 2, you will have   _____ ¢

If you add 1 more penny to
number 3, you will have   _____ ¢

**To count these cents
takes a lot of sense!**

Counting with
Dimes, Nickels and Pennies

(Use with page 194)

There is a bake sale at school today.
Be sure to bring Mary Money along!

Decide which one you want.

In the space below, draw enough
money to pay for it.

Counting with
Dimes, Nickels and Pennies
(Use with page 193)

1. Sharita chose the doughnut.
   Circle the money she needed.

_____ ¢

2. Robert loves brownies.
   Circle the money he needed.

_____ ¢

3. Tom had 3 of these.
   He had _____ ¢. He spent it all
   on something good. **Draw** it here.

Yum!

Name_____

Counting with
Dimes, Nickels and Pennies

"Sir Circle" counts coins!
How much money?
Count the coins.
Circle the set with more money.

Example		
12¢ ____ **21¢** ____	____ ____	____ ____

____ ____	____ ____	____ ____

____ ____	____ ____	____ ____

Name_____

Counting with
Dimes, Nickels and Pennies

Colorful Coins

Count the coins. Use the right color to circle the set of coins with the most money.

Example:

17¢ _____   **21¢** _____

red

_____   _____

green

_____   _____

yellow

_____   _____

brown

_____   _____

blue

_____   _____

orange

Counting with
Dimes, Nickels and Pennies

Smart Shoppers

Circle the coins to show the right amount.

Example:

 47¢

 29¢

32¢

44¢

16¢

23¢

38¢

Name_____

Counting with
Dimes, Nickels and Pennies

Join the Coins
Draw a line from the coins to the right amount.

Example:

25¢

16¢

26¢

13¢

45¢

15¢

21¢

25¢

20¢

18¢

9¢

18¢

15¢

6¢

24¢

14¢

15¢

17¢

Subtracting with Dimes, Nickels and Pennies

Earning money is fun! So is spending it!
See what the children buy with their money.

"X" the coins needed.
Write how much money is left.

José wants

10¢

He has

_____¢
is left

Catherine wants

12¢

She has

_____¢
is left

Subtracting with
Dimes, Nickels and Pennies

Andrew wants

31¢

He has

_____¢

is left

Sherry wants

14¢

She has

_____¢

is left

Robert wants

42¢

He has

Can Robert buy the truck? _____

Subtracting with Dimes, Nickels and Pennies

Pay the exact amount for each toy.

A.

Coins left: _____

Money left: _____ ¢

B.

Coins left: _____

Money left: _____ ¢

C. **Choose** a price between 30¢ and 40¢.
Write the price on the robot's tag.

Coins left: _____

Money left: _____ ¢

Quarters: Introduction

Presenting...
the Quarter!

Our first president,
George Washington, is on the **front**.

front   back

_____ quarter = _____ pennies

_____ quarter = _____ cents

_____ quarter = _____ ¢

Count these nickels by 5's.

Is this another way to make 25¢?

yes   no

Quarters: Introduction

Follow each path to see how many quarters Mike and Maria found.

The **bananas** cost **25¢** each. How many can they buy? _____

Mike
Monkey

Maria
Monkey

BANANAS
25¢

Maria found quarters to buy _____ bananas.

Mike found quarters to buy _____ bananas.

Quarters:
Combinations of 25 Cents

These are all ways to make **25¢**.

Color each coin.

2 dimes,
1 nickel

5 nickels

25
pennies

Quarters: Combinations of 25 Cents

Count the money.
Write the amount.
A **quarter** is worth **25¢**.

A.

_____ ¢

B.

_____ ¢

Both of these pockets **show 25¢**.

Quarters:
Combinations of 25 Cents

It costs 25¢ to catch a fish.
Circle each group of coins that makes 25¢.

How many fish
can I catch?

Draw and **color** the fish I can catch._____

Quarters:
More or Less Than 50 Cents

The tooth fairy left 2 quarters
for your shiny baby tooth.

How much money do you have?
Each quarter is worth 25¢.
Two quarters = 50¢

Color each toy you can buy.

49¢ 25¢ 72¢ 39¢ 45¢ 60¢ 5¢

Quarters:
More or Less Than 50 Cents

Some children had fun spending the
allowance they earned.
The boys bought some cars.

Terry paid 5¢ for each **blue** car.
Color Terry's cars **blue**.

How much did Terry pay for the **blue** cars?

_____ ¢

Lucas liked the **red** cars. They were the same
price. **Color** his cars **red**.

How much did Lucas pay for the **red** cars?

_____ ¢

Which boy paid more? _____

Quarters:
More or Less Than 50 Cents

Patty bought some pears at the store.
She paid **25¢** for **each pear**. **Color** the pears.

25¢ each

Draw the quarters she spent.

How much money did she spend? _____¢

Jennifer bought these bananas. She paid **10¢** for
each one. **Color** the bananas.

10¢ each

Draw the dimes she spent.

How much money did she spend? _____¢

Which girl spent less? _____

Counting with Quarters

These are some machines
that one quarters.

Color each machine you have to put
quarters into.

Circle the number of quarters you need.

I need _____ quarters to wash clothes.

I need _____ quarter(s) to
make a phone call.

Counting with Quarters

75¢

Drinks

I need _____ quarters to buy a drink.

$1.00

I need _____ quarters to buy a comic book.

50¢

50¢

I need _____ quarters to buy a frozen
fruit bar.

Hurry! It's melting!

Name_____

Counting with Quarters, Dimes, Nickels and Pennies

Count the money.
Start with the quarters. Then **count** the dimes, nickels and pennies.

A.

 25¢   35¢   40¢   41¢
_____   _____   _____   _____
                                  Total

B.

 25¢   35¢   36¢   37¢   38¢
_____   _____   _____   _____   _____

 39¢   40¢
_____   _____
            Total

Counting with Quarters, Dimes, Nickels and Pennies

Count the money.
Write the amount.
A **quarter** is worth **25¢**.

A.

_____¢   _____¢   _____¢   _____¢
                                      Total

B.

_____¢   _____¢   _____¢   _____¢
                                      Total

C. **Put** more than 50¢ in the bank. **Show** the coins.

_____¢
Total

Counting with Quarters, Dimes, Nickels and Pennies

Count the money.
Start with the quarters. Then **count** the dimes, nickels and pennies.

A.

____¢ ____¢ ____¢ ____¢ ____¢
                                  Total

B.

____¢ ____¢ ____¢ ____¢ ____¢ ____¢

____¢ ____¢
      Total

I'm counting my money. 25¢, 35¢, 45¢, 55¢, 60¢, 65¢, 66¢, 67¢.

C. **Solve** this puzzle.
What coins does Lizard have?

Counting with Quarters, Dimes, Nickels and Pennies

Count the money.
Start with the quarter.
Write the amount. _____

A.

_____ ¢

B.

_____ ¢

Counting with **Quarters,**
Dimes, Nickels and Pennies

Count the money.

Start with the quarter.
Write the amount.

A.

_____¢

B.

_____¢

Counting with Quarters, Dimes, Nickels and Pennies

Match the money with the amount.

          35¢

          36¢

          40¢

          27¢

          15¢

          21¢

          8¢

Good work!

Counting with Quarters, Dimes, Nickels and Pennies

Quarterback Attack
Count the coins. **Start** with the quarters.
Write the amount in each football.

Example:

45¢

Counting with Quarters, Dimes, Nickels and Pennies

(Use with page 222)

Carolyn and Marilyn are going to the beach for their vacation.

The twins wanted to buy some things to take along. They emptied their piggy banks.

Counting with Quarters, Dimes, Nickels and Pennies

(Use with page 221)

Cross off the money Carolyn and Marilyn used for:

Color the pails **pink**.

Cross off the money they used for:

Color the beach balls **red** and **yellow**.

Cross off the money they used for:

Color the beach towels **blue** and **green**.

Cross off the money they used for:

Color the sunglasses.
Did they have enough money?_____

Counting with Quarters, Dimes, Nickels and Pennies

You Make "**Cents**"

~~**Count**~~ the coins.

Do you have enough money to buy each toy?

Example:	You have...		yes or no
58¢		51¢	no
47¢		_____	_____
75¢		_____	_____
43¢		_____	_____
98¢		_____	_____
32¢		_____	_____
26¢		_____	_____
45¢		_____	_____

Counting with Quarters, Dimes, Nickels and Pennies

It is fun to buy things to keep your hair looking great!

How many of each coin do you need? **Write** 1, 2, 3 or 4.

	Quarters	Dimes	Nickels	Pennies

Adding and Comparing Amounts of Money

(Use with page 226)
Christopher was a good shopper.
He looked for the best prices when he
bought school supplies.

30¢   25¢

Circle and **color** the one he bought.

        _____ ¢

or

        _____ ¢

Name_____

Adding and Comparing
Amounts of Money
(Use with page 225)

   _____ ¢

or

  _____ ¢

_____

   _____ ¢

or

   _____ ¢

_____

 Draw the coins you think he spent for this notebook. Good job, Chris! **Spend wisely!**

How much? _____ ¢

Adding Nickels and Pennies
(Use with page 229)

You know how to add numbers when they are in a problem. **Can you add money the same way?**

When Gerald earns money and saves it in his bank, Mother always gives him 7¢ more because he is 7 years old. Gerald washed the dishes. He was given this money.

Cut and **glue** the 7¢ Mom gave him on this page and page 229.
Write the number problem.

$$\begin{array}{r} 25 \\ 7 \\ \hline 32 \end{array}$$

**This page left blank for
cutting lesson on reverse side.**

Adding Dimes and Nickels
(Use with page 227)

Gerald mopped the kitchen floor for 2 dimes, then put wax on it for 2 more dimes.

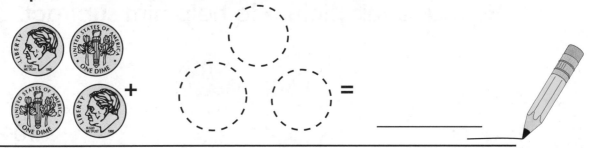

He watered all the plants.

He folded the clothes from the dryer and put them away.

Gerald is a hard worker!

Subtracting for Change

Adam wanted to know how
much change he would have left
when he bought things.

He made this picture to help him subtract.

```
  4 dimes
- 1 dime
```
3 dimes

```
  40¢
- 10¢
```
30¢

Cross out and subtract.

```
  6 dimes
- 4 dimes
```

```
  60¢
- 40¢
```

_____ dimes

Name_____

Coins

Subtracting for Change

Pay the exact amount for each toy.
Cross out the coins you use.

How much is left?

A.

16¢

Coins left: _____

Money left: _____ ¢

B.

20¢

Coins left: _____

Money left: _____ ¢

C.

25¢

Coins left: _____

Money left: _____ ¢

25¢

Subtracting for Change

Cross out. **Write** the problem.

Example:

Adam wants: Adam has:

$$
\begin{array}{r}
65\cancel{c} \\
-\ 60\cancel{c} \\
\hline
5\cancel{c}
\end{array}
$$

Adam wants: Adam has:

¢

-        ¢

_____

Adam wants: Adam has:

¢

-        ¢

_____

Name_____

Subtracting from 50 Cents

Maria went to the store to buy
a birthday gift for her best friend.

Maria took 50¢ to the store.
She looked at these things.

Circle the things she could buy.

Subtracting from 50 Cents

Maria wanted to know how much change she would get back from each toy.

16¢

```
  50¢
-    ¢
_____
```

29¢

```
  50¢
-    ¢
_____
```

32¢

```
  50¢
-    ¢
_____
```

36¢

```
  50¢
-    ¢
_____
```

Color the toy you think Maria chose.

Making Exact Amounts of Money

Use dimes, nickels and pennies.
Pay the exact amount for each toy.

A. What coins did you use?

_____ dimes _____ nickels

_____ pennies

B. What coins did you use?

_____ dimes _____ nickels

_____ pennies

C. **Solve** this puzzle.

What coins did Cat
use to pay for the ball?

_____ dimes _____ nickels

_____ pennies

Making Exact Amounts of Money

Use dimes, nickels and pennies.
Pay the exact amount for each toy.

A. What coins did you use?

_____ dimes   _____ nickels

_____ pennies

B. What coins did you use?

_____ quarters   _____ dimes

_____ nickels   _____ pennies

C. **Solve** this puzzle.

What coins did Alligator
use to pay for the
toothbrush?

I used three
coins to pay.

_____ dimes   _____ nickels

_____ pennies

Making Exact Amounts
of Money

Use quarters, dimes, nickels and pennies.
Pay the exact amount for each toy.

A. What coins did you use?

_____ quarters _____ dimes

_____ nickels _____ pennies

27¢

B. What coins did you use?

_____ quarters _____ dimes

_____ nickels _____ pennies

40¢

C. **Solve** this puzzle.

What coins did Bird use
to pay for the pilot wings?

_____ quarters _____ dimes

_____ nickels _____ pennies

I used 6 coins to pay.

PILOT WINGS 30¢

Making Exact Amounts of Money

Use quarters, dimes, nickels and pennies.
Pay the exact amount for each toy.

A. What coins did you use?

50¢

_____ quarters _____ dimes
_____ nickels _____ pennies

B. What coins did you use?

45¢

_____ quarters _____ dimes
_____ nickels _____ pennies

C. **Solve** this puzzle.

What coins did Frog use
to pay for the bow tie?

I used 4 coins to pay.

40¢

_____ quarters _____ dimes
_____ nickels _____ pennies

Making Exact Amounts of Money

Use quarters, dimes, nickels and pennies.
Pay the exact amount for each toy.

66¢

A. What coins did you use?

_____ quarters _____ dimes

_____ nickels _____ pennies

75¢

B. What coins did you use?

_____ quarters _____ dimes

_____ nickels _____ pennies

C. **Solve** this puzzle.

What coins did Rabbit use to pay for the watch?

I used 8 coins to pay.

53¢

_____ quarters _____ dimes

_____ nickels _____ pennies

Name _____

Making Exact Amounts of Money and Change

Use the coins shown.
Pay the exact amount for each toy.
How much do you have left?

A.

Coins left: _____

Money left: _____¢

B.

Coins left: _____

Money left: _____¢

C.

Choose a price between 42¢ and
58¢. **Write** the price on the tag.

Coins left: _____

Money left: _____¢

Problem-Solving with Money

(Use with page 244)
To be a good problem-solver,
you must **read the problem carefully**.

Think: What do I want to know?

plant
26¢

frog
15¢

car
14¢

7¢
ball

8¢
ring

horn
9¢

Solve these problems.

1.	2.
Buy a ⊙ ⸨8⸩¢	Buy a 🚗 ¢
Buy a ⚾ 7¢	Buy a 🎺 ¢
_____	_____
15	¢
How much for both the ring and the ball?	How much more for the car?
(Add) Subtract	Add (Subtract)

Problem-Solving with Money

(Use with page 243)

| 3. Buy a   ¢ | 4. Buy a   ¢ |

3. Buy a _____ ¢

Buy a _____ ¢

How much more for the plant?

Add   Subtract

4. Buy a _____ ¢

Buy a _____ ¢

How much for both the horn and the ring?

Add   Subtract

5. Buy a _____ ¢

Buy a _____ ¢

How much for both the ball and car?

Add   Subtract

6. Buy a _____ ¢

Buy a _____ ¢

How much more for the frog?

Add   Subtract

7. **Circle** the one which costs more.

8. **Circle** the one which costs more.

Buy a , a and a .

How much for all?

_____ ¢ + _____ ¢ + _____ ¢ = _____ ¢

Problem-Solving with Money

How Much?
Draw the coins you use.
Write the number of coins on each blank.

A.

9¢

⑤ ◯ ◯ ◯ ◯

_____ dimes
_____ nickels
_____ pennies

B.

11¢

_____ dimes
_____ nickels
_____ pennies

C.

14¢

_____ dimes
_____ nickels
_____ pennies

D. Find another way to pay for the

14¢

_____ dimes
_____ nickels
_____ pennies

Problem-Solving with Money

How Much?

Draw the coins you use.
Write the number of coins on each blank.

A.

13¢

_____ dimes
_____ nickels
_____ pennies

B.

15¢

_____ dimes
_____ nickels
_____ pennies

C.

18¢

_____ dimes
_____ nickels
_____ pennies

D. Find another way to pay for the

18¢

_____ dimes
_____ nickels
_____ pennies

Problem-Solving with Money

How much?

Draw the coins you use.
Write the number of coins on each blank.

A.

35¢

_____ quarters
_____ dimes
_____ nickels
_____ pennies

B.

29¢

_____ quarters
_____ dimes
_____ nickels
_____ pennies

C.

43¢

_____ quarters
_____ dimes
_____ nickels
_____ pennies

D. Find another way to pay for the

43¢

_____ quarters
_____ dimes
_____ nickels
_____ pennies

Problem-Solving with Money

How Much?

Draw the coins you use.
Write the number of coins on each blank.

A.

50¢

_____ quarters
_____ dimes
_____ nickels
_____ pennies

B.

66¢

_____ quarters
_____ dimes
_____ nickels
_____ pennies

C.

70¢

_____ quarters
_____ dimes
_____ nickels
_____ pennies

D. Find another way to pay for the

70¢

_____ quarters
_____ dimes
_____ nickels
_____ pennies

Making Exact Amounts of Money: Two Ways to Pay

Find two ways to pay.
Show what coins you use.

27¢

A.

_____ quarters
_____ dimes
_____ nickels
_____ pennies

B.

_____ quarters
_____ dimes
_____ nickels
_____ pennies

32¢

C.

_____ quarters
_____ dimes
_____ nickels
_____ pennies

D.

_____ quarters
_____ dimes
_____ nickels
_____ pennies

Making Exact Amounts of Money: Two Ways to Pay

Find two ways to pay.
Show what coins you use.

38¢

A.

_____ quarters
_____ dimes
_____ nickels
_____ pennies

B.

_____ quarters
_____ dimes
_____ nickels
_____ pennies

40¢

C.

_____ quarters
_____ dimes
_____ nickels
_____ pennies

D.

_____ quarters
_____ dimes
_____ nickels
_____ pennies

Making Exact Amounts of Money: Two Ways to Pay

Find two ways to pay.
Show what coins you use.

50¢

A.

_____ quarters
_____ dimes
_____ nickels
_____ pennies

B.

_____ quarters
_____ dimes
_____ nickels
_____ pennies

65¢

C.

_____ quarters
_____ dimes
_____ nickels
_____ pennies

D.

_____ quarters
_____ dimes
_____ nickels
_____ pennies

Making Exact Amounts of Money: How Much More?

Count the coins.
Find out how much more money you need to pay the exact amount.

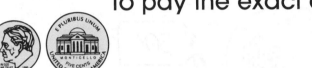

A.

How much money do you have? _____ ¢

How much more money do you need? _____ ¢

B.

How much money do you have? _____ ¢

How much more money do you need? _____ ¢

C. **Solve** this puzzle.

How much more
money does
Frog need?

_____ ¢

I have 1 quarter, 2 nickels, and 15 pennies. I need one more coin to buy the plane.

Making Exact Amounts of Money: How Much More?

Count the coins.
Find out how much more money you need to pay the exact amount.

A.

How much money do you have? _____ ¢

How much more money do you need? _____ ¢

B.

How much money do you have? _____ ¢

How much more money do you need? _____ ¢

C. **Solve** this puzzle.

How much more money does Monkey need?

_____ ¢

I have 1 quarter and 4 dimes. I need one more coin to pay for the banana-van.

75¢

Name_____

Half-Dollars: Introduction

Introducing the Half-Dollar

Meet another one of my
money friends... the **Half-Dollar!**

front

back

The half-dollar is worth 50¢.

Look at each side of the half-dollar.
Color them silver.

_____ half-dollar = _____ pennies

_____ half-dollar = _____ cents

_____ half-dollar = _____ ¢

Half-Dollars: Introduction

These are some ways to make a half dollar.
Color each coin.

 1 half-dollar

 2 quarters

10 nickels

 5 dimes

50 pennies

Counting Half-Dollars, Quarters, Dimes, Nickels and Pennies

Count the money.
Write each amount.
A **half-dollar** is worth **50¢** or **$.50**

A.

_____ _____ _____   _____¢

_____

B.

_____ _____ _____ _____   _____¢

_____

C. **Draw** between 50¢ and 90¢ in the jar.

Name_____

Counting Half-Dollars, Quarters, Dimes, Nickels and Pennies

Count the money.
Write each amount.

A.

_____ _____ _____   _____ ¢

B.

_____ _____ _____ _____ _____ ¢

C. **Draw** more than 80¢ in the pocket.

257

Counting Coins: How Much More?

Count the coins.
Find out how much more money you need to pay the exact amount.

A.

How much money do you have? _____ ¢

How much more money do you need? _____ ¢

B.

How much money do you have? _____ ¢

How much more money do you need? _____ ¢

C. **Solve** this puzzle.

How much more money does
Alligator need?

_____ ¢

I have 1 half-dollar and 1 quarter. I need one more coin to pay for the jump rope.

Name_____

Counting Coins:
How Much More?

Count the coins.
Find out how much more money you need
to pay the exact amount.

A.

How much money do you have? _____ ¢

How much more money do you need? _____ ¢

B.

How much money do you have? _____ ¢

How much more money do you need? _____ ¢

C. Solve this puzzle.

How much more money does
Raccoon need?

_____ ¢

I have 1 half-dollar, 1 quarter, 2 dimes, 1 nickel and 4 pennies. I need one more coin to buy the spyglass.

259

Dollar Bills: Introduction

Introducing the Dollar
Meet my friend, William Dollar.
I call him **Dollar Bill** for short!
Hee, Hee!

This is a **dollar bill**.

It has **2 sides**.

Color them **green**.

1 dollar = $1.00

1 dollar =   one dollar

1 dollar =   pennies

1 dollar = _____ cents

Dollar Bills: Introduction

Long ago, people got tired of
carrying heavy coins in their pockets,
so... dollar bills were made!

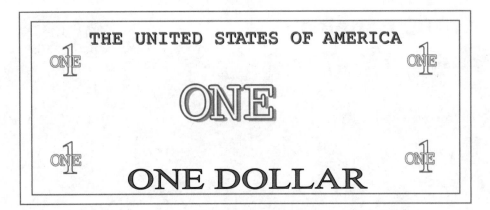

This is the **dollar sign**: **$**
It is an S with a line through it.

There is also a period between
the dollars and the cents: $1.00

Name_____

Dollar Bills: Introduction

There are many ways to make a dollar.

1 dollar bill

2 half-dollars

4 quarters

100 pennies

Dollar Bills: Introduction

Here are some more ways to make a dollar!

Count each set of coins.
If it equals one dollar, **write** $1.00 on the line.

Count by 10's with dimes. _____

Count by 5's with nickels. _____

It's a lot easier to carry **1 dollar bill** than **20 nickels!**

Counting with
Dollar Bills and Coins

Writing Dollar Amounts

A few **dollar tips** for you...
1. Drop the ¢ sign.
2. Add the $ sign.
3. Use a . (period) between the dollars and cents.

Write the amount of dollars and cents.

 1.

$ _____1.08_____

2.

$ _____._____

Counting with Dollar Bills and Coins

Count the money.
Write each amount.

A one-dollar bill is worth 100¢ or $1.00.

A.

____ ____ $ _____1.25

_____

B.

____ ____ ____ $ _____

_____

C. Draw about $2.00 in the bank. **Use** a one-dollar bill.

Name_____

Counting with Dollar Bills and Coins

Count the money.
Write each amount.

1.

$ _____._____

2.

THE UNITED STATES OF AMERICA
ONE DOLLAR

THE UNITED STATES OF AMERICA
ONE DOLLAR

$ _____._____

3.

$ _____._____

4.

$ _____._____

Matching Dollar Amounts

Count the money.
Draw a line to match.

$1.07

$1.37

$1.32

$1.12

Name_____

Coins and Bills

Matching Dollar Amounts

A Good Match

Count the money.
Draw a line to match.

$1.26

$1.27

$ .86

$1.21

Example

$1.75

$1.81

$1.03

$1.25

$1.65

$1.10

$1.02

$1.06

$1.07

$1.01

$ .78

268

Name_____

Coins and Bills

Counting Dollar Bills and Coins: How Much More?

Count the coins and bills.
Find out how much more money
you need to pay the exact amount.

A.

How much money do you have? _____¢

How much more money do
you need? _____¢

B.

How much money do you have? _____¢

How much more money do you need? _____¢

C. **Solve** this puzzle.

How much more money
does Anteater need?

_____¢

I have 1 dollar bill, 1
quarter, 1 dime and 1 penny.
I need one more coin to
buy the flashlight.

$1.61

269

Name_____

Estimating Amounts of Money

We estimate, or round up or down,
to make a quick guess about money.

Circle the amount that is closer to the amount
on the tag. **This is an estimate.**

39¢

(about 40¢)

about 30¢

38¢

about 30¢

about 40¢

42¢

about 30¢

about 40¢

about 50¢

Name_____

Estimating Amounts of Money
Circle the best estimate.

 $1.49

about 50¢

about $1.40

about $1.50

 $2.98

about $2.00

about $3.00

about $4.00

 $1.98

about $1.00

about $2.00

about $3.00

 $3.05

about $3.00

about $4.00

271

Name_____

Adding and Subtracting Amounts of Money: Using Estimation

Using estimation makes it much easier to add or subtract in your head.

These foods are for sale in the lunchroom.

 39¢   21¢   19¢   11¢   29¢

You have this much money:

You want the **Round or estimate** the cost. _____ ¢

Do you have enough money?_____

The and look good.

Add the estimated prices.

You probably have enough!

Adding and Subtracting Amounts of Money: Using Estimation

You have this money:

You have _____ cents.

If you buy , will you have enough left to buy

a 🍌 ?

               yes   no

money you have =   _____¢

estimated milk =   - _____¢

                              _____¢

You have this money:

You want to buy 🥛 and an 🍎 .

Estimate.

Do you have enough money? _____

Which other fruit can you buy to have with your milk?

_____

Name_____

Adding and Subtracting Amounts of Money: Making Change

How much change should you get?

Example:

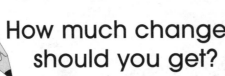

Bought:		**I have:**

```
        29¢       55¢
      + 14¢     - 43¢
      _____    _____
        43¢       12¢
```

Change **12¢**

Bought:		**I have:**

```
        56¢
      + 27¢
      _____
```

Change ☐

Bought:		**I have:**

```
        61¢
      + 59¢
      _____
```

Change ☐

Bought:		**I have:**

```
       $ .78
      +$ .69
      _____
```

Change ☐

Bought:		**I have:**

```
       $ .59
      +$ .86
      _____
```

Change ☐

Bought:		**I have:**

```
       $ .66
      + $ .75
      _____
```

Change ☐

Name_____

Adding and Subtracting Amounts of Money: Making Change

Lunch Money
How much change?

Example:

Lunch:	I have:
59¢	115¢
+ 17¢	- 76¢
76¢	39¢
	Change 39¢

Lunch:	I have:
$ .86	
+ $ .15	
	Change

Lunch:	I have:
$0.75	
+ $ .16	
	Change

Lunch:	I have:
$ .66	
+ $1.26	
	Change

Lunch:	I have:
77¢	
+ 54¢	
	Change

Lunch:	I have:
64¢	
+ 89¢	
	Change

Making Change: Money Puzzles

Solve the puzzles.
Show how much change you get.

A. Use 2 quarters.

Pay 45¢

What change will
you get? _____

B. Use 1 quarter, 2 dimes
and 2 nickels.

Pay 53¢

What change will
you get? _____

C. Use 3 quarters
and 1 dime.

Pay 76¢

What change will
you get? _____

D. Use 3 quarters and
2 nickels.

Pay 82¢

What change will
you get? _____

Making Change: Money Puzzles

Solve the puzzles.
Show how much change you get.

A. Use 1 one-dollar bill.

Pay 75¢

What change will
you get? _____

B. Use 1 half-dollar and
2 quarters.

Pay 90¢

What change will
you get? _____

C. Use 1 one-dollar bill
and 1 quarter.

Pay 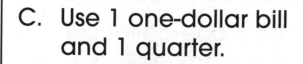 $1.10

What change will
you get? _____

D. Use 2 half-dollars, 1
quarter and 1 dime.

Pay $1.30

What change will
you get? _____

Making Change: Money Puzzles

Solve the puzzles.
Show how much change you get.

A. Use 3 half-dollars.

Pay $1.12

What change will
you get? _____

**B. Use 1 one-dollar bill,
2 quarters and 1 dime.**

Pay $1.54

What change will
you get? _____

**C. Use 1 one-dollar bill, 1
half-dollar and 1
quarter.**

 $1.68

Pay

What change will
you get? _____

**D. Use 1 one-dollar bill
and 2 half-dollars.**

Pay $1.51

What change will
you get? _____

Making Change: Money Puzzles

Solve the puzzles.
Show how much change you get.

A. Use 2 one-dollar bills.

Pay $1.59

What change will
you get? _____

B. Use 2 one-dollar bills.

Pay $1.85

What change will
you get? _____

C. Use 3 one-dollar bills.

Pay $2.65

What change will
you get? _____

D. Use 3 one-dollar bills.

Pay $2.06

What change will
you get? _____

Making Change: Money Puzzles

Solve the puzzles.
Show how much change you get.

A. Use 4 one-dollar bills.

Pay

What change will
you get? _____

B. Use 5 one-dollar bills.

Pay

What change will
you get? _____

C. Use 3 one-dollar bills.

Pay

What change will
you get? _____

D. Use 2 one-dollar bills.

Pay

What change will
you get? _____

Making Exact Amounts of Money

Pay for each toy.
Show what coins you use.

A.

60¢

_____ quarters

_____ dimes

_____ nickels

B.

55¢

_____ quarters

_____ dimes

_____ nickels

C. **Write** the price.

¢

_____ quarters

_____ dimes

_____ nickels

Making Exact Amounts
of Money

Pay for each snack.
Show what coins you use.

A.

65¢

_____ quarters
_____ dimes
_____ nickels
_____ pennies

B.

49¢

_____ quarters
_____ dimes
_____ nickels
_____ pennies

C. **Write** the price.

_____ quarters
_____ dimes
_____ nickels
_____ pennies

Making Exact Amounts of Money

Pay for each robot.
Show what coins you use.

A.

85¢

_____ half-dollars
_____ quarters
_____ dimes
_____ nickels
_____ pennies

B.

$1.00

_____ half-dollars
_____ quarters
_____ dimes
_____ nickels
_____ pennies

C. Write the price.

_____ half-dollars
_____ quarters
_____ dimes
_____ nickels
_____ pennies

Making Exact Amounts of Money

Pay for each animal.
Show what coins you use.

A.

$1.50

_____ half-dollars
_____ quarters
_____ dimes
_____ nickels
_____ pennies

B.

$1.35

_____ half-dollars
_____ quarters
_____ dimes
_____ nickels
_____ pennies

C. Write the price.

_____ half-dollars
_____ quarters
_____ dimes
_____ nickels
_____ pennies

Coins and Bills

Making Exact Amounts of Money

Pay for each toy.
Show what money you use.

A.

$1.30

_____ dollars
_____ half-dollars
_____ quarters
_____ dimes
_____ nickels
_____ pennies

B.

$1.55

_____ dollars
_____ half-dollars
_____ quarters
_____ dimes
_____ nickels
_____ pennies

C. Write the price.

_____ dollars
_____ half-dollars
_____ quarters
_____ dimes
_____ nickels
_____ pennies

Name_____

Making Exact Amounts of Money

Pay for each game.
Show what money you use.

A.

$1.05

_____ dollars
_____ half-dollars
_____ quarters
_____ dimes
_____ nickels
_____ pennies

B.

$1.75

_____ dollars
_____ half-dollars
_____ quarters
_____ dimes
_____ nickels
_____ pennies

C. Write the price.

_____ dollars
_____ half-dollars
_____ quarters
_____ dimes
_____ nickels
_____ pennies

Using Combinations of Coins to Pay

How Would You Pay?
Pay for each cookie.
Use as few coins as you can.

					Number of Coins Used
A. 28¢	1			3	4
B. 39¢					
C. 49¢					
D. Write the price. ___ ¢					

Using Combinations of Coins to Pay

How Would You Pay?
Pay for each toy.
Use as few coins as you can.

					Number of Coins Used
A. 22¢					
B. 37¢					
C. 52¢					
D. Write the price. ___¢					

288

Using Combinations of Coins to Pay

How Would You Pay?
Pay for each book.
Use as few coins as you can.

					Number of Coins Used
A. SUPER 75¢					
B. SPORT 80¢					
C. Monster 97¢					
D. Write the price. MAGIC ___¢					

Using Combinations of Coins to Pay

How Would You Pay?
Pay for each snack.
Use as few coins as you can.

					Number of Coins Used
A. popcorn **$1.05**					
B. ice cream cone **95¢**					
C. popsicle **85¢**					
D. Write the price. drink					

Name_____

Using Combinations of Coins to Pay

How Would You Pay?
Pay for each mask.
Use as few coins and bills as you can.

	ONE				Number of Coins Used
A. $1.75					
B. $1.95					
C. $2.50					
D. Write the price.					

Making Exact Amounts of Money Two Ways

Find two ways to pay for each thing.
Pay the exact amount.

A.

40¢

	Dimes	Nickels	Pennies
Way 1	4		
Way 2		8	

B.

34¢

	Dimes	Nickels	Pennies
Way 1			
Way 2			

C. Write a price for the magnifying glass.

	Dimes	Nickels	Pennies
Way 1			
Way 2			

Making Exact Amounts of Money Two Ways

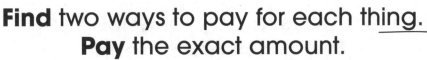

Find two ways to pay for each thing.
Pay the exact amount.

A. 52¢

	Quarters	Dimes	Nickels	Pennies
Way 1				
Way 2				

B. 75¢

	Quarters	Dimes	Nickels	Pennies
Way 1				
Way 2				

C. **Write** a price for the game.

	Quarters	Dimes	Nickels	Pennies
Way 1				
Way 2				

Making Exact Amounts of Money Two Ways

Find two ways to pay for each thing.
Pay the exact amount.

STICK-ON JEWELS $1.25

A.

	Half-Dollars	Quarters	Dimes	Nickels	Pennies
Way 1					
Way 2					

B.

$1.50

	Half-Dollars	Quarters	Dimes	Nickels	Pennies
Way 1					
Way 2					

C. **Write** a price for the robot.

	Half-Dollars	Quarters	Dimes	Nickels	Pennies
Way 1					
Way 2					

Name_____

Making Exact Amounts of Money Two Ways

Find two ways to pay for each thing.
Pay the exact amount.

$1.00

A.

	$1 Bills	Half-Dollars	Quarters	Dimes	Nickels
Way 1					
Way 2					

B.

$1.65

	$1 Bills	Half-Dollars	Quarters	Dimes	Nickels
Way 1					
Way 2					

$2.45

C. Solve this puzzle.
What's missing in each way?

	$1 Bills	Half-Dollars	Quarters	Dimes	Nickels
Way 1	2			2	
Way 2		4	1		

Making Exact Amounts of Money Two Ways

Find two ways to pay for each thing.
Pay the exact amount.

$5.60

A.

	$1 Bills	Half-Dollars	Quarters	Dimes	Nickels	Pennies
Way 1						
Way 2						

$5.95

B.

	$1 Bills	Half-Dollars	Quarters	Dimes	Nickels	Pennies
Way 1						
Way 2						

C.

$6.72

Solve this puzzle.
What's missing in each way?

	$1 Bills	Half-Dollars	Quarters	Dimes	Nickels	Pennies
Way 1	5	1				12
Way 2	4		1			7

Estimating Amounts of Money

Snacks

banana	pudding	popcorn	cookies	crackers & peanut butter
10¢	25¢	30¢	20¢	15¢

Use the coins shown.
If you spend all your money, which snacks can you buy? **First**, estimate. **Then**, check.

A.

I think I can buy: _____

I can buy: _____

B.

I think I can buy: _____

I can buy: _____

C. **Solve** this puzzle.

Ahmad had 1 quarter, 1 dime, 1 nickel
and 10 pennies. He bought two snacks.
He has less than 10 cents left.
What snacks did he buy? _____

Estimating Amounts of Money

Pet Treats

BEEF MUNCHIES 25¢ BIRD SEED 65¢ HAMSTER DONUTS 50¢ DOG COOKIES 55¢ KITTY TREATS 75¢ TURTLE Delight 35¢

Use the coins shown.
If you spend all your money, which pet treats
can you buy? **First**, estimate. **Then**, check.

A.

I think I can buy: _____
I can buy: _____

B.

I think I can buy: _____
I can buy: _____

C. **Solve** this puzzle.
Ismelda had 3 half-dollars. She bought 3 pet
treats. She has less than 20 cents left.
What treats did she buy?_____

Name_____

Estimating Amounts of Money

Fun Fair Tickets

HAUNTED HOUSE $0.50 POWER UP $0.45 RIDE-A-LLAMA $0.75 TREASURE HUNT $0.25 WAVE POOL $1.00 sea SUB $0.35

Use the coins and bills shown.
If you spend all your money, what tickets can
you buy? **First,** estimate. **Then,** check.

A.

I think I can buy: _____
I can buy: _____

B.

I think I can buy: _____
I can buy: _____

C. **Solve** this puzzle.
Larry and Leticia had 2 one-dollar bills and 3
half-dollars. They bought 6 tickets. They used all
of their money. What tickets did they buy?

_____

Estimating Amounts of Money

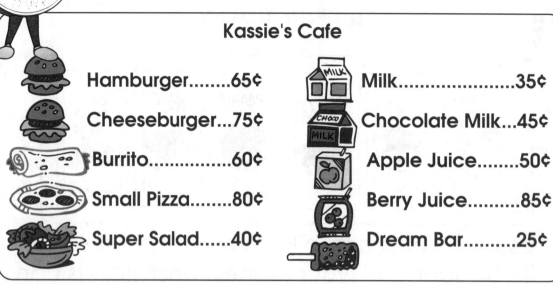

Kassie's Cafe

Hamburger........65¢

Cheeseburger...75¢

Burrito...............60¢

Small Pizza........80¢

Super Salad......40¢

Milk.......................35¢

Chocolate Milk...45¢

Apple Juice........50¢

Berry Juice..........85¢

Dream Bar..........25¢

Use the coins and bills shown.
If you spend all your money, what can you buy?
First, estimate. **Then,** check.

A.

I think I can buy:_____

I can buy: _____

B.

I think I can buy:_____

I can buy: _____

C. **Solve** this puzzle.
Tina had 1 one-dollar bill, 1 half-dollar and 2
quarters. She bought three things. She has less than
25 cents left. What did Tina buy?_____

Estimating Amounts of Money

Whale of a Sale - Birthday Gifts

eraser	pen	patch	keyring	button	cards	jug
$1.00	$1.10	$0.75	$0.85	$0.25	$1.20	$1.50

Use the coins and bills shown.
If you spend all your money, what can you buy?
First, estimate. **Then,** check.

A.

I think I can buy: _____

I can buy: _____

B.

I think I can buy: _____

I can buy: _____

C. **Solve** this puzzle.
Martin had 3 one-dollar bills.
He bought three gifts. He has less than 25 cents left.
What did Martin buy?_____

Making Exact Amounts and Change

Pay the exact amount.
What change do you get back?

A.

Amount you get back:

_____ ¢

B.

Amount you get back:

_____ ¢

C.

Amount you get back:

_____ ¢

Making Exact Amounts and Change

Pay the exact amount.
What change do you get back?

A.

Amount you get back:

_____ ¢

B.

Amount you get back:

_____ ¢

C.

Choose a price between
75¢ and 90¢. **Write** the price.

Amount you get back:

_____ ¢

Making Exact Amounts and Change

Pay the exact amount.
What change do you get back?

A.

Amount you get back:

_____ ¢

$0.81

B.

Amount you get back:

_____ ¢

$1.05 JUMBO CRAYONS

C.

Choose a price between $1.15
and $1.28. **Write** the price.

Amount you get back:

_____ ¢

Making Exact Amounts and Change

Pay the exact amount.
What change do you get back?

A.

$1.26

Amount you get back: _____ ¢

B.

$2.67

Amount you get back: _____ ¢

C. **Solve** this puzzle.

What did Abby pay?
Write the amount on the tag.

I had 2 one-dollar bills.
I paid for the kite. I got
back a quarter, 1 dime
and 1 penny.

Making Exact Amounts and Change

Pay the exact amount.
What change do you get back?

A.

Amount you get back: $_____

B.

Amount you get back: $_____

C. **Solve** this puzzle.

What did Dominic pay?
Write the amount on the tag.

I had five one-dollar bills. I paid for the compass. I got back 2 one-dollar bills, 1 quarter and 3 pennies.

Money Puzzles

Solve the puzzles.
Draw the coins.

A. There are 4 coins in the bag. Together they are worth less than 50¢. What coins could they be?	**B.** There are 4 coins in the bag. Two are worth more than 25¢ each. Two are worth less than 10¢ each. What coins could they be?
C. There are 5 coins in the bag. Together they are worth more than 90¢. What coins could they be?	**D.** There are 6 coins in the bag. Together they are worth between 75¢ and $1.00. What coins could they be?

Money Puzzles

Solve the puzzles.
Draw the coins.

A. There are 5 coins in the bank. Together they are worth $1.00 exactly. What coins could they be?	B. There are 6 coins in the bank. Together they are worth between 80¢ and $1.20. What coins could they be?
C. There are 6 coins in the bank. Two are worth more than 10¢ each. Four are worth less than 10¢ each. All together they are worth more than $1.00. What coins could they be?	D. There are 6 coins in the bank. Four are worth more than 10¢ each. Two are worth less than 25¢ each. All together they are worth less than $1.50. What coins could they be?

Using Combinations of Coins to Pay

Use the coins shown to make each amount.

A. Use 3 of the coins to make 25¢. What coins did you use?			2	1	
B. Use 4 of the coins to make 50¢. What coins did you use?					
C. Use 4 of the coins to make 66¢. What coins did you use?					
D. Use 5 of the coins to make 96¢. What coins did you use?					

Using Combinations of Coins to Pay

Use the coins shown to make each amount.

A. Use 3 of the coins to make 60¢. What coins did you use?				
B. What other way can you do it?				
C. Use 4 of the coins to make 40¢. What coins did you use?				
D. What other way can you do it?				
E. Use 4 of the coins to make 80¢. What coins did you use?				
F. What other way can you do it?				

Name_____

Money Story Puzzles

Solve the money story puzzles.

A. Sean sees a box of magnets on sale for 50 cents. He takes 10 coins out of his pocket and buys the magnets.

What coins could they be?

B. Tonia sees a small bag of jacks for 58 cents. She takes 9 coins out of her pocket to pay.

What coins could they be?

C. Dustin sees a toy hammer. He wants to buy it for his little brother. He pulls six coins out of his pocket and pays 75 cents.

What coins could they be?

Money Story Puzzles

Solve the money story puzzles.

A. Matt buys a box of things for doing magic tricks. He takes an even number of coins out of his pocket and pays 65 cents.

What coins could they be?

B. Stacey buys a poster for 70 cents. She uses an odd number of coins to buy it.

What coins could they be?

C. **Write** a money story puzzle about buying the stuffed whale.

Money Story Puzzles

Solve the money story puzzles.

A. Amber put coins into her bank for a
    long time. She saved $6.25 in all.
    Amber saved $3.55 more than her
    sister Holly.

    How much did Holly save?

B. Collin and Jason each bought a
    watch. Jason paid $4.99 for his
    Flip-up Crocodile Watch. That was
    $1.20 more than Collin paid for his
    Dinosaur Watch.

    How much did Collin pay?

C. **Write** a money story puzzle
    about yourself and a friend.

Money Story Puzzles

Solve the money story puzzles.

A. Darci and Kara fed the horses at the fair. Kara's mother gave the girls 3 one-dollar bills, 3 quarters, 5 dimes and 3 nickels. Darci and Kara divided the money equally.

How much money did each of them get?

B. Josh and Ben washed cars one Saturday. When they finished, they had 3 one-dollar bills, 1 1 half dollar, three quarters, 2 dimes and 1 nickel in their money box. The boys divided the money fairly.

How much money did each of them get?

C. **Write** a money story puzzle about earning money and dividing it equally.

Money Story Puzzles

Solve the money story puzzles.

A. Eric and Alicia took all the coins out of their pockets. They put the coins together and paid 65 cents for a bag of corn chips. Alicia paid 15 cents more than Eric.

How much did each of them pay?

B. Two friends put their money together and bought a package of stickers for $1.60. Rachel paid 20 cents more than Amanda.

How much did each girl pay?

C. **Write** a money story puzzle about buying something with a friend.

Coins and Dollar Bills

Time Award Certificates

Champion Time Teller!

_____
name

You are a champion time teller because_____

_____

Nice Going!

Signed_____ Date_____

_____
name

Wonderful Work!

You are wonderful because_____

_____

Way to Go!

Signed_____ Date_____

Money Award Certificates

Math Marvel!

_____
name

You are a Math Marvel because _____

_____

Marvelous Job!

Signed _____ Date _____

_____
name

Wonderful Work!

You are a Money Expert because _____

_____

Awesome Work!

Signed_____ Date _____

Page 6

Page 7

Page 8

Page 9

Page 10

Page 11

Page 12

Page 13

Page 14

Page 15

Page 16

Page 17

Page 18

Page 19

Page 20

Page 21

Page 22

Page 23

Page 24

Page 25

Page 26

Page 27

Page 28

Page 29

Page 30

Page 31

Page 32

Page 33

Page 34

Page 35

Page 36

Page 37

Page 38

Page 39

Page 40

Page 41

Page 42

Page 43

Page 44

Page 45

Page 46

Page 47

Page 48

Page 49

Page 50

Page 51

Page 52

Page 53

Page 54

Page 55

Page 56

Page 57

Page 58

Page 59

Time Lapse: Hours

It is important to get home when your parents expect you!

Steve went to play baseball at **3:30**. Mom told him to be home in **2 hours**.

He should be home at __5__ : __30__.
Show the time on this watch.

Tiffany went to Latonia's house to ride bikes at **10:00**. Dad asked her to be home in **3 hours**.

She should be home at __1__ : __00__.
Show the time on this watch.

Page 60

Time Lapse: Hours

Kristen took her sister to the movies at **7:30**. Mom said she would meet them in **2 hours**.

She will meet them at __9__ : __30__.
Show the time on this clock.

Latrissa went to the library for story hour. She got there at **1:00**. She stayed **1 hour**.

Story hour should be over at __2__ : __00__.
Show the time Latrissa left for home.

Page 61

**Drawing the Hour Hand:
A Half-Hour Later**

Draw the hands on each clock face.

A. At **7:00**, Bill turns on the TV.

What time is it one half-hour later?

B. At **4:00**, we all jump in the car.

What time is it one half-hour later?

C. At **12:00**, Julio and Nathan are ready to eat.

What time is it one half-hour later?

Page 62

**Drawing the Hour Hand:
A Half-Hour Later**

Draw the hands on each clock face.

A. At **8:00**, it starts to rain.

What time is it one half-hour later?

B. At **11:00**, the sun comes out.

What time is it one half-hour later?

C. At **3:00**, we skip home from school.

What time is it one half-hour later?

Page 63

**Drawing the Hour Hand:
A Half-Hour Later**

Draw the hands on each clock face.

A. At **6:30**, a fire engine roars down the street.

What time is it one half-hour later?

B. At **11:30**, everyone is playing in the schoolyard.

What time is it one half-hour later?

C. At **5:30**, my dog gets out of the yard.

What time is it one half-hour later?

Page 64

Time Stories

Read each story.
Draw the hands on each clock face.

A. Tom makes a HUGE sandwich at **1:00**. He finishes the whole sandwich **one half-hour** later. What time does Tom finish the sandwich?

B. Tom gets home from school at **3:00**. He goes out to play **30 minutes** later. What time does Tom go out to play?

C. Tom goes to bed at **8:30**. He falls asleep **one half-hour** later. What time does Tom fall asleep?

Page 65

Time Stories

Read each story.
Draw the hands on each clock face.

A. Maria makes a lunch at **7:00**. She gets on the bus **30 minutes** later. What time does she get on the bus?

B. Maria helps make dinner at **5:30**. Everyone eats it **one half-hour** later. What time does everyone eat?

C. Maria's family plays a game at **8:30**. They stop playing **30 minutes** later. What time do they stop playing?

Page 66

Time Stories

Read each story.
Draw the hands on each clock face.

A. Li goes for a walk at **10:30**. He comes back with three friends **30 minutes** later. What time does he come back with his friends?

B. Li gets on his bike at **3:30**. He reaches the library **one half-hour** later. What time does he get to the library?

C. Li starts home at **5:00**. He gets home **30 minutes** later. What time does he get home?

Page 67

Time Two Ways

Draw the hands on each clock face.
Write the time.

A. At **1:30**, Squirrel hides seven nuts.

`1:30`

B. At **2:00**, Squirrel runs down the tree to find more nuts.

`2:00`

C. By **3:30**, Squirrel is ready for a long rest.

`3:30`

Page 68

Time Two Ways

Time to the Half-Hour

Draw the hands on each clock face.
Write the time.

A. At **5:30**, Toad hops over to visit Frog.

5:30

B. At **6:00**, Frog and Toad are sipping Fine Fly Tea.

6:00

C. At **7:30**, Toad heads home, full of tea and bug cakes.

7:30

Page 69

Time Two Ways

Time to the Half-Hour

Draw the hands on each clock face.
Write the time.

A. Maria Mouse gets to the library at **11 o'clock**. She leaves the library at **11:30**.

Gets to library   **Leaves the library**

11:00   11:30

B. Marcus Mouse gets to Pizza Palace at **3 o'clock**. He finishes his pizza at **3:30**.

Gets to Pizza Palace   **Finishes pizza**

3:00   3:30

Page 70

Time Two Ways

Time to the Half-Hour

Draw the hands on each clock face.
Write the time.

A. Tim Toad begins planting the garden at **9 o'clock**. He finishes planting at **9:30**.

Begins planting   **Finishes planting**

9:00   9:30

B. Tara Toad starts roller-skating at **10 o'clock**. She stops roller-skating **30 minutes after 10 o'clock**.

Starts roller-skating   **Stops roller-skating**

10:00   10:30

Page 71

Time Two Ways

Time to the Half-Hour

Draw the hands on each clock face.
Write the time.

A. Ricardo Raccoon starts his lunch at **12:00**. He finishes his lunch **30 minutes after 12:00**.

Starts lunch   **Finishes lunch**

12:00   12:30

B. Rachel Raccoon sits down at the computer at **7:00**. She gets up from the computer a **half-hour after 7:00**.

Sits down   **Gets up**

7:00   7:30

Page 72

Time Stories

Time to the Half-Hour

Read the story.
Write the time two ways.
Choose a time for everyone to eat lunch!

Bear is going on a picnic today with his brother and sister. They leave for the park at 9:00. They get to the park at 10:00. Bear helps carry the food to a picnic table. Then he gets out his kite. Bear flies his kite at 10:30. Later, at (Answer will vary), everyone has a picnic lunch!
Put the story in order by writing what time Bear did each thing.

A. Leave for the park   B. Get to the park

9:00   10:00

C. Fly kite   D. Eat lunch

10:30   Answer will vary.

Page 73

Time Stories

Time to the Half-Hour

Read the story.
Write the time two ways.
Choose a time for everyone to go home!

Pig wakes up at 7:00. Pig's grandmother is taking her to the zoo today! They get to the zoo at 10:30. They walk and walk. They stop to eat at 12:30. They walk some more. Pig and her grandmother don't get home until (Answers will vary). They had a wonderful day!
Put the story in order by writing what time Pig did each thing.

A. Wakes up   B. Get to zoo

7:00   10:30

C. Stop to eat   D.

12:30   Answer will vary.

Page 74

Time Stories

Time to the Half-Hour

Read the story.
Write the time two ways.
Choose a time for everyone to wake up!

It's a hot summer day. Frog and Turtle begin to walk to the lake at 11:00. They jump into the cold water at 12:30. They swim and dive. They enjoy lunch at 1:30. They fall asleep after lunch. Later, at (Answers will vary), Frog and Turtle wake up. They hurry home!
Put the story in order by writing what time Frog and Turtle did each thing.

A. Walk to the lake   B. Jump into water

11:00   12:30

C. Have lunch   D.

1:30   Answers will vary.

Page 75

Time Puzzles

Time to the Half-Hour

Read each "time clue."
Draw the hands on each clock.
Write the time.

Answers will vary.

A. It's dark outside. Everyone is asleep.

B. Ring, ring! Time to get up.

C. Here comes the school bus. Run, so you won't be late!

D. I'm hungry! Soon it will be time for lunch.

Page 76

Time Puzzles

Time to the Half-Hour

Read each "time clue."
Draw the hands on each clock.
Write the time.

Answers will vary.

A. School is out! We're going home.

B. Here comes the mail! I hope I get a letter.

C. It's getting dark. Time to go inside.

D. It's light tonight. Look, a big full moon!

Page 77

Page 78

Page 79

Page 80

Page 81

Page 82

Page 83

Page 84

Page 85

Page 86

Page 87

Page 88

Page 89

Page 90

Page 91

Page 92

Page 93

Page 94

Page 95

Page 96

Page 99

Page 100

Page 101

Page 102

Page 103

Page 104

Page 105

Page 106

Page 107

Page 108

Page 109

Page 110

Page 111

Page 112

Page 113

Page 114

Page 115

Drawing Clock Hands

Show the Times
Read each story.
Draw the hands on each clock face.

A. Rabbit hops into his garden at 6:00. He finishes working in the garden one and one-half hours later.

Hops in garden **Finishes work**

B. Rabbit gets out lettuce and carrots at 8:30. He finishes eating 45 minutes later.

Gets out lettuce & carrots **Finishes eating**

C. Rabbit lies down for a nap at 4:00. He wakes up and hip-hops away 55 minutes later.

Lies down **Wakes up**

Page 116

Drawing Clock Hands

Show the Times
Read each story.
Draw the hands on each clock face.

A. Pig takes a mud bath at 9:00. Pig showers off 15 minutes later.

Takes mud bath **Showers off**

B. On Monday, Pig begins cleaning at noon. Her house is clean and neat 90 minutes later.

Begins cleaning **House is clean**

C. On Tuesday, Pig goes to the market at 12:45. She comes home with a basket full of goodies 30 minutes later.

Goes to market **Comes home**

Page 117

Time Stories

Read the story.
Write the times on each digital clock.

Val and Phil Camp Out

Val and Phil go out to the backyard at 6:00. They put up their tent. This takes them 1 hour and 30 minutes. They get in the tent and talk for 1 hour. Then they fall asleep. They sleep for 2 hours, until a dog barks and wakes them up.

A. Go to backyard **6:00**   B. Finish putting up tent **7:30**

C. Fall asleep **8:30**   D. Dog barks **10:30**

E. How long are Val and Phil in the yard before the dog wakes them up?
4 hours **30** minutes

Page 118

Time Stories

Read the story.
Write the times on each digital clock.

Mike and Maria Go Skating

Mike and Maria leave home at 3:30. They ride their bikes to the ice-skating rink. This takes one half-hour. They skate and leave the rink 2 hours later. They get on their bikes and arrive home 40 minutes after leaving the rink.

A. Leave home **3:30**   B. Get to rink **4:00**

C. Leave rink **6:00**   D. Arrive home **6:40**

E. How long does Mike & Maria's trip to the skating rink and back take?
3 hours **10** minutes

Page 119

Time Stories

Read the story.
Write the times on each digital clock.

Joe and José Go Skating

Joe and José put on roller skates at 8:30. They skate for 2 hours, then stop to rest. They rest for one half-hour, then start skating again. They reach the park 1 hour and 45 minutes later.

A. Put on roller skates **8:30**   B. Stop to rest **10:30**

C. Start skating again **11:00**   D. Get to park **12:45**

E. How long does Joe and José's trip to the park take?
4 hours **15** minutes

Page 120

Time Stories

Read each time story.
Write the time on each clock.

Andrea took her dog for a walk. They left home at 5:30. They walked for 20 minutes. What time did they get home?

A. Leave home **5:30**   B. Get home **5:50**

Rhiannon and her mother were making cookies. They put the cookies in the oven at 7:15. After 10 minutes they took the cookies out of the oven. Yum! What time did they take them out?

C. Cookies in oven **7:15**   D. Cookies out of oven **7:25**

Solve the time puzzle.
When did Anita begin playing ping-pong? Anita played ping-pong with her brother for 30 minutes. They stopped playing at 4:30.

E. Begin playing **4:00**   F. Stop playing **4:30**

Page 121

Time Stories

Read each time story.
Write the time on each clock.

Benito went for a ride on the roller coaster. He got on the roller coaster at 2:30. He rode for 15 minutes. What time did he get off?

A. Start ride **2:30**   B. Get off **2:45**

Valerie and her sister went hiking. They started hiking at 9:00. They hiked for one hour and 30 minutes. What time did they stop hiking?

C. Start hike **9:00**   D. Finish hike **10:30**

Solve this time puzzle.
When did Ben and his mother get on the subway? Ben and his mother rode the subway for 20 minutes. They got off the subway at 4:30.

E. Get on **4:10**   F. Get off **4:30**

Page 122

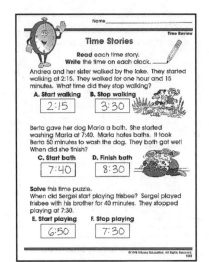

Time Stories

Read each time story.
Write the time on each clock.

Andrea and her sister walked by the lake. They started walking at 2:15. They walked for one hour and 15 minutes. What time did they stop walking?

A. Start walking **2:15**   B. Stop walking **3:30**

Berta gave her dog Maria a bath. She started washing Maria at 7:40. Maria hates baths. It took Berta 50 minutes to wash the dog. They both got wet! When did she finish?

C. Start bath **7:40**   D. Finish bath **8:30**

Solve this time puzzle.
When did Sergei start playing frisbee? Sergei played frisbee with his brother for 40 minutes. They stopped playing at 7:30.

E. Start playing **6:50**   F. Stop playing **7:30**

Page 123

Time Puzzles

Write any time that fits the time clues.

A. Between 11:00 and 12:00   *Answers will vary.*

B. Between 30 minutes after 2:00 and 3:00

C. After quarter-past 7:00 and before 8:00

D. **Make** up your own time clues.
Ask a friend to solve your time puzzle!

Page 124

Page 125

Name_____

Time Puzzles

Write any time that fits the time clues.

A. Between 4:15 and 5:15   *Answers will vary.*

[:]

B. After 6:00 and before quarter to 7:00

[:]

C. Between noon and 1:00

[:]

D. **Make up** your own time clues.
Ask a friend to solve your time puzzle!

_____
_____
_____

Page 126

Name_____

Time Puzzles

Write any time that fits the time clues.

A. After 3:00 and before 3:40   *Answers will vary.*

[:]

B. Between quarter after 1:00 and 3:00

[:]

C. Before 9:00 and after 8:20

[:]

D. **Make up** your own time clues.
Ask a friend to solve your time puzzle!

Page 127

Name_____

Time Stories

Read the story. **Write** the time on each clock.

Story Times

Erin and her brother Harry were shopping for dinner. First they went into the bakery at 5:00 to buy fresh bread. This took 5 minutes. Next they walked to the market for vegetables and cereal. This took them 20 minutes. Then they walked next door for a treat at Fanny's Famous Fudge. This took them 15 minutes. Then they met their brother Andrew outside.

A. Go into bakery   **5:00**   C. Leave bakery   **5:05**

B. Leave market   **5:25**   D. See Andrew   **5:40**

E. **How long** had Erin and Harry been shopping when they saw Andrew?
40 minutes

F. **Make up** your own story about shopping. What do you do, and how long does each thing take? Make up a starting time. Use your clock to find the ending time.

Page 128

Name_____

Time Stories

Read the story. **Write** the time on each clock.

Story Times

Hanna and Shawn got to the fair at 3:00. They threw balls at the clown's pocket for 10 minutes. No luck! Then they rode the Big Dipper for 30 minutes. They got wet! After this they ate pizza for 15 minutes. Then they saw their friend Mary.

A. Go to fair   **3:00**   B. Stop throwing balls   **3:10**

C. Stop riding Big Dipper   **3:40**   D. See Mary   **3:55**

How long had Hanna and Shawn been at the fair when they saw Mary?
55 minutes

E. **Make up** your own story about being at a fair. What do you do, and how long does each thing take? Make up a starting time. Use your clock to find the ending time.

Page 129

Name_____

Time Stories

Read the story. **Write** the time on each clock.

Story Times

A. Valerie and Angela got off the bus at the mall. It was 12:30. First they went to Toby's Toys & Games. They looked at toys for 20 minutes. Then they spent 40 minutes walking to Yummy Yogurt and having a snack. Then they looked at shoes in The Shoe Factory for 15 minutes. They met Angela's sister outside the Shoe Factory.

A. Go to mall   **12:30**   B. Leave toy store   **12:50**

C. Leave Yummy Yogurt   **1:30**   D. See Angela's sister   **1:45**

E. **How long** had Valerie and Angela been at the mall when they saw Angela's sister?
1 hour and 15 minutes

F. **Make up** your own story about being at a mall. What do you do, and how long does each thing take? Make up a starting time. Use your clock to find the ending time.

Page 130

Name_____

Telling Time: Using Charts

BIG TEN MOVIES:

Mark's Great Adventure	12:15	3:00	5:30
The Mad Hatter Returns	12:45	3:30	5:45
Morris and the Magic Van	1:30	4:15	6:45

Use the chart.
Write the time that each pair went to a movie.

A. Barry and his brother went to the movie that began closest to 4:00.
Movie: *Morris and the Magic Van*
Began at: *4:15*

B. Andrea and her friend went to the movie that began closest to 1:00.
Movie: *The Mad Hatter Returns*
Began at: *12:45*

C. Ismelda and her mom went to the movie that began closest to 6:00.
Movie: *The Mad Hatter Returns*
Began at: *5:45*

D. **Make up** your own time puzzle about Big Ten Movies.

Page 131

Name_____

Telling Time: Using Charts

MAIN AIRPORT

MONDAY DEPARTURES:

Gull Air	10:45	12:10	1:45
Far West Airlines	9:25	10:10	11:40
Swift Flights	12:30	1:15	2:20

Use the chart.
Write the time that each pair took a flight.

A. Teresa and her aunt flew on the plane that left closest to 10:30.
Airline: *Gull Air*
Left at: *10:45*

B. Kelly and her mother flew on the plane that left closest to 11:00.
Airline: *Gull Air*
Left at: *10:45*

C. Leticia and her father flew on the plane that left closest to 12:15.
Airline: *Swift Flights*
Left at: *12:30*

D. **Make up** your own time puzzle about the Main Airport.

Page 132

Name_____

Telling Time: Using Charts

BAYSIDE AQUARIUM

SATURDAY FEEDINGS:

Otters	2:00	3:30	5:00
Dolphins	11:30	3:15	5:20
Sharks	2:30	4:00	5:45

Use the chart.
Write the time that each pair went to a feeding.

A. Francisco and José went to the feeding that was closest to 3:00.
Animal: *dolphins*
Feeding at: *3:15*

B. Alex and Shannon went to the feeding that was closest to 6:00.
Animal: *sharks*
Feeding at: *5:45*

C. Kim and Amanda went to the feeding that was closest to 5:30.
Animal: *dolphins*
Feeding at: *5:20*

D. **Make up** your own time puzzle about the Bayside Aquarium.

Page 134

Page 135

Page 136

Page 137

Page 138

Page 139

Page 140

Page 141

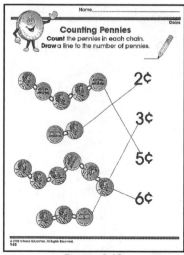

Page 142

Page 143

Name_____

Coins

Counting Pennies

Count the pennies in each triangle.

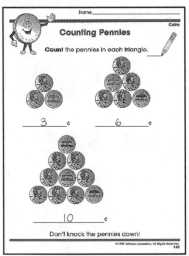

3 ¢   6 ¢

10 ¢

Don't knock the pennies down!

Page 144

Name_____

Coins

Counting Pennies

I put my pennies in bags.
Write the number of pennies on each bag.
Color each penny.

6¢

5¢

Page 145

Name_____

Coins

Counting Pennies

Count the pennies in each group.
Match it to the correct bag.

5¢

3¢

1¢

Don't lose your penny bag!

2¢

4¢

Page 146

Name_____

Coins

Counting Pennies

I love to go to the amusement park and ride rides.

Count the pennies.
Write the number of pennies on the line.
Color each ride.

4 ¢

Do you like the ferris wheel?

7 ¢

...the till-a-whirl?

Page 147

Name_____

Coins

Counting Pennies

...the merry-go-round?

3 ¢

...the water flume?

5 ¢

...the bumper cars?

5 ¢

Page 148

Name_____

Coins

Counting Pennies

A **penny** is worth 1¢.
Count the money. How much?

A.

2 ¢

B.

4 ¢

Page 149

Name_____

Coins

Counting Pennies

Count the money. How much?

A.

5 ¢

B.

6 ¢

Page 150

Name_____

Coins

Counting Pennies
Who Has More Money?

Count the money.
Write the amount.

A.

3 ¢

B.

7 ¢

C. **Circle** the answer.
Who has more money?

Page 151

Name_____

Coins

Nickels: Introduction

Meet another **money friend.**
Let's hear it for the **Nickel!**

silver

silver

Look at the two sides of a nickel.
Color the nickels silver.

front   back

1 nickel = 5 pennies

1 nickel = 5 cents

1 nickel = 5 ¢

5¢ = 1¢ + 1¢ + 1¢ + 1¢ + 1¢

=

334

Page 152

Page 153

Page 154

Page 155

Page 156

Page 157

Page 158

Page 159

Page 160

Page 161

Page 162

Page 163

Page 164

Page 165

Page 166

Page 167

Page 168

Page 169

Page 170

Page 171

Page 172

Page 173

Page 174

Page 175

Page 176

Page 177

Page 178

Page 179

Page 180

Page 181

Page 182

Page 183

Page 184

Page 185

Page 186

Page 187

Page 188

Page 189

Page 190

Page 191

Page 192

Page 193

Page 194

Page 195

Page 196

Page 197

Page 198

Page 199

Page 200

Page 201

Page 202

Page 203

Page 204

Page 205

Page 206

Page 207

Page 208

Page 209

Page 210

Page 211

Page 212

Page 213

Page 214

Page 215

Page 216

Page 217

Page 218

Page 219

Page 220

Page 221

Page 222

Page 223

Page 224

Page 225

Page 226

Page 227

Page 229

Page 230

Page 231

Page 232

Page 233

Page 234

Name_____

Subtracting from 50 Cents

Maria wanted to know how much change she would get back from each toy.

yo-yo	16¢	50¢ - 16¢ **34¢**
party hat	29¢	50¢ - 29¢ **21¢**
bear	32¢	50¢ - 32¢ **18¢**
worm	36¢	50¢ - 36¢ **14¢**

Color the toy you think Maria chose.

Page 235

Name_____

Making Exact Amounts of Money

Use dimes, nickels and pennies.
Pay the exact amount for each toy.

A. What coins did you use?
1 dimes _____ nickels
_____ pennies (10¢)

B. What coins did you use?
1 dimes **1** nickels
4 pennies (19¢)

C. **Solve** this puzzle.
What coins did Cat use to pay for the ball?
1 dimes **1** nickels
_____ pennies (15¢)

Page 236

Name_____

Making Exact Amounts of Money

Use dimes, nickels and pennies.
Pay the exact amount for each toy.

A. What coins did you use?
2 dimes _____ nickels
1 pennies (21¢)

B. What coins did you use?
1 quarters **1** dimes
_____ nickels **2** pennies (37¢)

C. **Solve** this puzzle.
What coins did Alligator use to pay for the toothbrush?
I used three coins to pay.
1 dimes **2** nickels
_____ pennies (20¢)

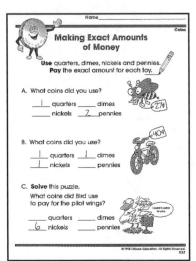

Page 237

Name_____

Making Exact Amounts of Money

Use quarters, dimes, nickels and pennies.
Pay the exact amount for each toy.

A. What coins did you use?
1 quarters _____ dimes
_____ nickels **2** pennies (27¢)

B. What coins did you use?
1 quarters **1** dimes
1 nickels _____ pennies (40¢)

C. **Solve** this puzzle.
What coins did Bird use to pay for the pilot wings?
I used 6 coins to pay.
_____ quarters _____ dimes
6 nickels _____ pennies

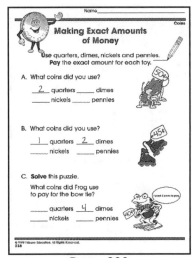

Page 238

Name_____

Making Exact Amounts of Money

Use quarters, dimes, nickels and pennies.
Pay the exact amount for each toy.

A. What coins did you use?
2 quarters _____ dimes
_____ nickels _____ pennies (50¢)

B. What coins did you use?
1 quarters **2** dimes
_____ nickels _____ pennies (45¢)

C. **Solve** this puzzle.
What coins did Frog use to pay for the bow tie?
I used 5 coins to pay.
_____ quarters **4** dimes
_____ nickels _____ pennies

Page 239

Name_____

Making Exact Amounts of Money

Use quarters, dimes, nickels and pennies.
Pay the exact amount for each toy.

A. What coins did you use?
2 quarters **1** dimes
_____ nickels **6** pennies (66¢)

B. What coins did you use?
3 quarters _____ dimes
_____ nickels _____ pennies (75¢)

C. **Solve** this puzzle.
What coins did Rabbit use to pay for the watch?
I used 8 coins to pay.
_____ quarters **5** dimes
_____ nickels **3** pennies (53¢)

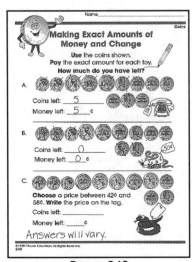

Page 240

Name_____

Making Exact Amounts of Money and Change

Use the coins shown.
Pay the exact amount for each toy.
How much do you have left?

A.
Coins left: **5**
Money left: **5** ¢

B.
Coins left: **0**
Money left: **0** ¢

C. **Choose** a price between 42¢ and 58¢. **Write** the price on the tag.
Coins left: _____
Money left: _____ ¢

Answers will vary.

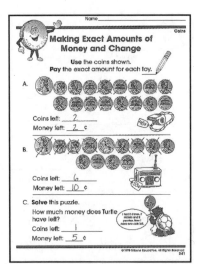

Page 241

Name_____

Making Exact Amounts of Money and Change

Use the coins shown.
Pay the exact amount for each toy.

A.
Coins left: **2**
Money left: **2** ¢

B.
Coins left: **6**
Money left: **10** ¢

C. **Solve** this puzzle.
How much money does Turtle have left?
Coins left: **1**
Money left: **5** ¢

Page 242

Name_____

Making Exact Amounts of Money and Change

Use the coins shown.
Pay the exact amount for each toy.

A.
Coins left: **0**
Money left: **0** ¢

B.
Coins left: **15**
Money left: **15** ¢

C. **Solve** this puzzle.
How much money does Squirrel have left?
Coins left: **1**
Money left: **25** ¢

Page 243

Page 244

Page 245

Page 246

Page 247

Page 248

Page 249

Page 250

Page 251

Making Exact Amounts of Money: How Much More?

Count the coins.
Find out how much more money you need to pay the exact amount.

A. How much money do you have? _15_ ¢
How much more money do you need? _10_ ¢

B. How much money do you have? _38_ ¢
How much more money do you need? _7_ ¢

C. **Solve** this puzzle.
How much more money does Frog need?
_5_ ¢

Page 252

Making Exact Amounts of Money: How Much More?

Count the coins.
Find out how much more money you need to pay the exact amount.

A. How much money do you have? _25_ ¢
How much more money do you need? _25_ ¢

B. How much money do you have? _11_ ¢
How much more money do you need? _49_ ¢

C. **Solve** this puzzle.
How much more money does Monkey need?
_10_ ¢

Page 253

Half-Dollars: Introduction

Introducing the Half-Dollar!

Meet another one of my money friends... the **Half-Dollar!**

front — silver — back

The half-dollar is worth 50¢.

Look at each side of the half-dollar.
Color them silver.

_1_ half-dollar = _50_ pennies
_1_ half-dollar = _50_ cents
_1_ half-dollar = _50_ ¢

Page 254

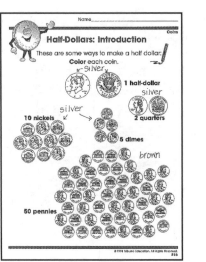

Half-Dollars: Introduction

These are some ways to make a half dollar.
Color each coin.

silver — 1 half-dollar
silver — 2 quarters
10 nickels — 5 dimes
brown
50 pennies

Page 255

Counting Half-Dollars, Quarters, Dimes, Nickels and Pennies

Count the money.
Write each amount.
A **half-dollar** is worth **50¢ or $.50**

A. _50_ _60_ _70_   _70_ ¢

B. _50_ _75_ _85_ _90_   _90_ ¢

C. **Draw** between 50¢ and 90¢ in the jar.
Answers will vary.

Page 256

Counting Half-Dollars, Quarters, Dimes, Nickels and Pennies

Count the money.
Write each amount.

A. _50_ _75_ _85_   _85_ ¢

B. _50_ _60_ _70_ _75_ _76_   _76_ ¢

C. **Draw** more than 80¢ in the pocket.
Answers will vary.

Page 257

Counting Coins: How Much More?

Count the coins.
Find out how much more money you need to pay the exact amount.

A. How much money do you have? _75_ ¢
How much more money do you need? _15_ ¢

B. How much money do you have? _70_ ¢
How much more money do you need? _29_ ¢

C. **Solve** this puzzle.
How much more money does Alligator need?
_1_ ¢

Page 258

Counting Coins: How Much More?

Count the coins.
Find out how much more money you need to pay the exact amount.

A. How much money do you have? _75_ ¢
How much more money do you need? _25_ ¢

B. How much money do you have? _1.00_ ¢
How much more money do you need? _29_ ¢

C. **Solve** this puzzle.
How much more money does Raccoon need?
_5_ ¢

Page 259

Dollar Bills: Introduction

Introducing the Dollar

Meet my friend, William Dollar.
I call him **Dollar Bill** for short!
Hee, Hee!

This is a **dollar bill.**
It has **2 sides.**
Color them green.

THE UNITED STATES OF AMERICA
ONE
ONE DOLLAR

1 dollar = $1.00
1 dollar = _one dollar_
1 dollar = _100_ pennies
1 dollar = _100_ cents

Page 260

Page 263

Page 264

Page 265

Page 266

Page 267

Page 268

Page 269

Page 270

Page 271

Page 272

Page 273

Page 274

Page 275

Page 276

Page 277

Page 278

Page 279

Page 280

Making Exact Amounts of Money

Pay for each toy.
Show what coins you use.

A. 60¢ — **2** quarters / **1** dimes / ___ nickels

B. 55¢ — **2** quarters / ___ dimes / **1** nickels

C. **Write** the price. *Answers will vary.*
___ quarters / ___ dimes / ___ nickels

Page 281

Making Exact Amounts of Money

Pay for each snack.
Show what coins you use.

A. 65¢ — ___ quarters / **6** dimes / **1** nickels / ___ pennies

B. 49¢ — ___ quarters / **4** dimes / **1** nickels / **4** pennies

C. **Write** the price. *Answers will vary.*
___ quarters / ___ dimes / ___ nickels / ___ pennies

Page 282

Making Exact Amounts of Money

Pay for each robot.
Show what coins you use.

A. 85¢ — **1** half-dollars / **1** quarters / **3** dimes / **1** nickels / ___ pennies

B. $1.00 — **2** half-dollars / ___ quarters / ___ dimes / ___ nickels / ___ pennies

C. **Write** the price. *Answers will vary.*
___ half-dollars / ___ quarters / ___ dimes / ___ nickels / ___ pennies

Page 283

Making Exact Amounts of Money

Pay for each animal.
Show what coins you use.

A. $1.50 — **3** half-dollars / ___ quarters / ___ dimes / ___ nickels / ___ pennies

B. $1.35 — **2** half-dollars / **1** quarters / **3** dimes / ___ nickels / ___ pennies

C. **Write** the price. *Answers will vary.*
___ half-dollars / ___ quarters / ___ dimes / ___ nickels / ___ pennies

Page 284

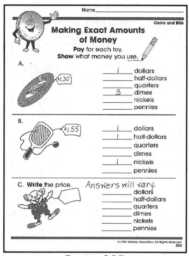

Making Exact Amounts of Money

Pay for each toy.
Show what money you use.

A. $1.30 — **1** dollars / ___ half-dollars / ___ quarters / **3** dimes / ___ nickels / ___ pennies

B. $1.55 — **1** dollars / **1** half-dollars / ___ quarters / ___ dimes / **1** nickels / ___ pennies

C. **Write** the price. *Answers will vary.*
___ dollars / ___ half-dollars / ___ quarters / ___ dimes / ___ nickels / ___ pennies

Page 285

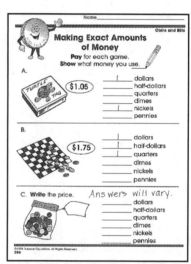

Making Exact Amounts of Money

Pay for each game.
Show what money you use.

A. $1.05 — **1** dollars / ___ half-dollars / ___ quarters / ___ dimes / ___ nickels / ___ pennies

B. $1.75 — **1** dollars / **1** half-dollars / **1** quarters / ___ dimes / ___ nickels / ___ pennies

C. **Write** the price. *Answers will vary.*
___ dollars / ___ half-dollars / ___ quarters / ___ dimes / ___ nickels / ___ pennies

Page 286

Using Combinations of Coins to Pay

How Would You Pay?
Pay for each cookie.
Use as few coins as you can.

				Number of Coins Used
A. 28¢	1		3	4
B. 39¢	1	1	4	6
C. 49¢	1	2	4	7
D. Write the price. ___¢	*Answers will vary.*			

Page 287

Using Combinations of Coins to Pay

How Would You Pay?
Pay for each toy.
Use as few coins as you can.

				Number of Coins Used
A. 22¢		2	2	4
B. 37¢	1	1	2	4
C. 52¢	2		2	4
D. Write the price. ___¢	*Answers will vary.*			

Page 288

Using Combinations of Coins to Pay

How Would You Pay?
Pay for each book.
Use as few coins as you can.

				Number of Coins Used
A. 75¢	3			3
B. 80¢	3	1		4
C. 97¢	3	2	2	7
D. Write the price. ___¢	*Answers will vary.*			

Page 289

Page 290

Page 291

Page 292

Page 293

Page 294

Page 295

Page 296

Page 297

Page 298

Page 299

Page 300

Page 301

Page 302

Page 303

Page 304

Page 305

Page 306

Page 307

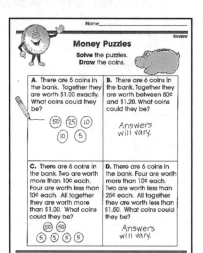

Money Puzzles

Solve the puzzles.
Draw the coins.

A. There are 5 coins in the bank. Together they are worth $1.00 exactly. What coins could they be?

(50) (25) (10)
(10) (5)

B. There are 6 coins in the bank. Together they are worth between 80¢ and $1.20. What coins could they be?

Answers will vary.

C. There are 6 coins in the bank. Two are worth more than 10¢ each. Four are worth less than 10¢ each. All together they are worth more than $1.00. What coins could they be?

(50) (50)
(5) (5) (5) (5)

D. There are 6 coins in the bank. Four are worth more than 10¢ each. Two are worth less than 25¢ each. All together they are worth more than $1.50. What coins could they be?

Answers will vary.

Page 308

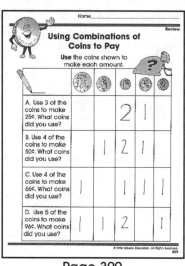

Using Combinations of Coins to Pay

Use the coins shown to make each amount.

	🪙	🪙	🪙	🪙
A. Use 3 of the coins to make 25¢. What coins did you use?			2	1
B. Use 4 of the coins to make 50¢. What coins did you use?		1	2	1
C. Use 4 of the coins to make 66¢. What coins did you use?	1	1	1	1
D. Use 5 of the coins to make 96¢. What coins did you use?	1	1	2	1

Page 309

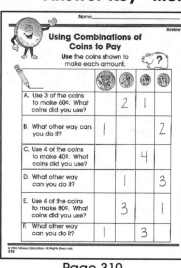

Using Combinations of Coins to Pay

Use the coins shown to make each amount.

	🪙	🪙	🪙	🪙
A. Use 3 of the coins to make 60¢. What coins did you use?		2	1	
B. What other way can you do it?	1			2
C. Use 4 of the coins to make 40¢. What coins did you use?			4	
D. What other way can you do it?		1		3
E. Use 4 of the coins to make 80¢. What coins did you use?		3		1
F. What other way can you do it?	1		3	

Page 310

Money Story Puzzles

Solve the money story puzzles.

A. Sean sees a box of magnets on sale for 50 cents. He takes 10 coins out of his pocket and buys the magnets.
What coins could they be?
nickels

B. Tonia sees a small bag of jacks for 58 cents. She takes 9 coins out of her pocket to pay.
What coins could they be?
(10) (10) (10) (10) (10) (5) (1) (1) (1)

C. Dustin sees a toy hammer. He wants to buy it for his little brother. He pulls six coins out of his pocket and pays 75 cents.
What coins could they be?
(25) (10) (10) (10) (10) (10)

Page 311

Money Story Puzzles

Solve the money story puzzles.

A. Matt buys a box of things for doing magic tricks. He takes an even number of coins out of his pocket and pays 65 cents.
What coins could they be?
Answers will vary.

B. Stacey buys a poster for 70 cents. She uses an odd number of coins to buy it.
What coins could they be?
Answers will vary.

C. Write a money story puzzle about buying the stuffed whale.
Answers will vary.

Page 312

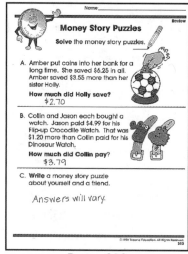

Money Story Puzzles

Solve the money story puzzles.

A. Amber put coins into her bank for a long time. She saved $6.25 in all. Amber saved $3.55 more than her sister Holly.
How much did Holly save?
$2.70

B. Collin and Jason each bought a watch. Jason paid $4.99 for his Flip-up Crocodile Watch. That was $1.20 more than Collin paid for his Dinosaur Watch.
How much did Collin pay?
$3.79

C. Write a money story puzzle about yourself and a friend.
Answers will vary.

Page 313

Money Story Puzzles

Solve the money story puzzles.

A. Darci and Kara fed the horses at the fair. Kara's mother gave the girls 3 one-dollar bills, 3 quarters, 5 dimes and 3 nickels. Darci and Kara divided the money equally.
How much money did each of them get?
$2.20

B. Josh and Ben washed cars one Saturday. When they finished, they had 3 one-dollar bills, 1 half dollar, three quarters, 2 dimes and 1 nickel in their money box. The boys divided the money fairly.
How much money did each of them get?
$2.25

C. Write a money story puzzle about earning money and dividing it equally.
Answers will vary.

Page 314

Money Story Puzzles

Solve the money story puzzles.

A. Eric and Alicia took all the coins out of their pockets. They put the coins together and paid 65 cents for a bag of corn chips. Alicia paid 15 cents more than Eric.
How much did each of them pay?
Eric paid 25¢. Alicia paid 40¢.

B. Two friends put their money together and bought a package of stickers for $1.60. Rachel paid 20 cents more than Amanda.
How much did each girl pay?
Amanda paid 70¢.
Rachel paid 90¢.

C. Write a money story puzzle about buying something with a friend.
Answers will vary.

Page 315

COINS

10¢
10 cents
dime

50¢
50 cents
half-dollar

5¢
5 cents
nickel

1¢
1 cent
penny

25¢
25 cents
quarter

MONEY

$5.00
five
dollars

$20.00
twenty
dollars

$1.00
one
dollar

$10.00
ten
dollars